Famous Biographies for Young People

BOOKS BY CHARLEMAE ROLLINS

Christmas Gif'
They Showed the Way
Famous American Negro Poets

FAMOUS AMERICAN NEGRO POETS

by Charlemae Rollins

ILLUSTRATED

Dodd, Mead & Company · New York

Printed in the United States of America
by Vail-Ballou Press, Inc., Binghamton, N. Y.

J 928
R

Grateful acknowledgment is made for permission to use the poems from the following sources: "A Black Man Talks of Reaping" and "The Day Breakers" by Arna Bontemps, from *American Negro Poetry*, copyright 1963, by Hill and Wang, Publishers, reprinted by permission of the author; From *Bronzeville Boys and Girls* by Gwendolyn Brooks, "DeKoven," copyright © 1956 by Gwendolyn Brooks Blakely, "Gertrude," copyright © 1956 by Gwendolyn Brooks Blakely, "Jim" copyright © 1956 by Gwendolyn Brooks Blakely, reprinted by permission of Harper and Row, Publishers, Incorporated; From *On These I Stand* by Countee Cullen, "Incident," copyright 1925 by Harper and Brothers, renewed 1953 by Ida M. Cullen, "Black Majesty," copyright 1929 by Harper and Brothers, renewed 1957 by Ida M. Cullen, reprinted by permission of Harper and Row, Publishers, Incorporated, "Ere Sleep Comes Down to Soothe the Weary Eyes," "In The Morning," and "Little Brown Baby," by Paul Laurence Dunbar, reprinted by permission of Dodd, Mead and Company, from *The Complete Poems of Paul Laurence Dunbar;* "Come, Come assist me, truant muse!" "Why Stirs With Sad Alarm the Heart," "Westward the Course of Empire Takes its Way," reprinted by permission of Dodd, Mead and Company from *Paul Laurence Dunbar and His Song* by Virginia Cunningham, copyright 1947, by Virginia Cunningham; "Merry-Go-Round," "Mother to Son" and "The Negro Speaks of Rivers," by Langston Hughes, from *Selected Poems of Langston Hughes,* copyright 1959 by Alfred A. Knopf, Inc., reprinted by permission of the author and publisher. "Organ Grinder," "Sky Pictures," "Sassafras Tea," by Effie Lee Newsome, from *Gladiola Garden,* copyright 1940, reprinted by permission of The Associated Publishers; "For Mary McLeod Bethune," by Margaret Walker, reprinted by permission of the author; "Big John Henry," "Childhood," "Lineage," and "For My People," by Margaret Walker, from *For My People,* copyright 1942, reprinted by permission of Yale University Press. "Go Down Death" by James Weldon Johnson, from *God's Trombones* by James Weldon Johnson, copyright 1927 by The Viking Press, Inc., 1955 by Grace Nail Johnson, reprinted by permission of The Viking Press, Inc.

This book is affectionately dedicated to the Children, the Parents, and the Teachers who eagerly searched for information about Negro Poets at The George Cleveland Hall Branch of The Chicago Public Library.

ACKNOWLEDGMENTS

The author wishes to thank the following poets for checking their biographies for accuracy and for generously providing their favorite photographs; Arna Bontemps, Gwendolyn Brooks, Langston Hughes, Effie Lee Newsome, and Margaret Walker.

Also special thanks to Dr. Benjamin F. Quarles, President of The Associated Publishers, Inc., for providing the photographs of Frances E. W. Harper, James Weldon Johnson, and Phillis Wheatley, and to Mrs. Ida Cullen Harper for sharing some personal recollections of Countee Cullen.

I am deeply grateful to my friends, Margaret Taylor Burroughs, Bertha S. Jenkinson, and Margaret Thomsen Raymond for editorial assistance in preparing the biographies presented here, and to Josephine Glover Sanders for patiently typing the many versions of the sketches.

Charlemae Rollins

CONTENTS

Illustrations follow page 32

INTRODUCTION

From the earliest beginnings of the United States, Negroes have made valuable contributions to the field of poetry. Although Phillis Wheatley, a slave girl, was the first American woman to publish a complete volume of poetry, the very first poem recorded by a Negro woman in America is attributed to a slave named Lucy Terry, who was owned by Ensign Ebenezer Wells of Deerfield, Massachusetts. It is quite a long narrative poem called *Bars Fight*, an account of an early Indian raid on Deerfield, in 1746. The following stanza is quoted as being a genuine example of a story in verse.

> Eleazer Hawks was killed outright
> Before he had time to fight,
> Before he did the Indians see
> Was shot and killed immediately;
> Oliver Amsden he was slain
> Which caused his friends much grief and pain.
> Samuel Amsden they found dead
> Not many rods off from his head.

Just as the medieval troubadors, minstrels, bards and minnesingers carried throughout their lands the songs and poems of the people of that period, so did the Negro slaves preserve and spread their cultural heritage through the medium of spoken verse and songs. The "pattern" is the same as that of the Negro spiritual, a question and answer form or "call and 'sponse" (response), as it was commonly known.

The earliest slaves from Africa brought to America with them their chants and songs. Many of the traditional poems, stories, singing games, proverbs, and other examples of folklore have been traced and collected. These may be found through many sources today. One of the best known of the old-timers is a "call and 'sponse" or question and answer poem, *Did You Feed My Cow?*

"Did you feed my cow?"
Yes, Ma'am
"Will you tell me how?"
Yes, Ma'am
"How did you feed her?"
Corn and hay
"How did you feed her?"
Corn and hay.
"Did you milk her good?"
Yes, Ma'am
"Did you do like you should?"
Yes, Ma'am
"How did you milk her?"
Swish, swish, swish
"How did you milk her?"
Swish, swish, swish!
"Did that cow die?"
Yes, Ma'am
"With a pain in her eye?"
Yes, Ma'am

"How did she die?"
>Umph! Umph! Umph!
"How did she die?"
>Umph! Umph! Umph!
"Did the buzzards come?"
>Yes, Ma'am
"For to pick her bones?"
>Yes, Ma'am
"How did they come?"
>Flop! Flop! Flop!
"How did they come?"
>Flop! Flop! Flop!

There are others which have the rabbit as a hero, similar to the popular star of Joel Chandler Harris' *Brer Rabbit* stories. One is *Old Mister Rabbit*.

Old Mister Rabbit
He had a mighty habit,
Sneakin' in my garden
Eatin' my potatoes,
My ripe tomatoes,
Gnawin' at my cabbage,
And if he won't stop
I'm goin' to put him in the pot,
Yes, if he don't quit,
Goin' to fry him in the skillet.

Another hip-hopping favorite is *Mister Rabbit! Mister Rabbit!*

"Mister Rabbit! Mister Rabbit!
Your coat's mighty gray?"

"Yes, my friend, it was made that way."
"Mister Rabbit, Mister Rabbit
Your ears mighty long?"
"Yes, my friend they are put on wrong."
"Mister Rabbit, Mister Rabbit,
Your feet mighty red."
"Yes, my friend, I'm almost dead!"
"Mister Rabbit, Mister Rabbit,
Your tail's mighty white."
"Yes, my friend, I'm going to take it ought of sight!"

This anthology, *Famous American Negro Poets*, presents a selection of poets and poems of special interest to children and young people. It is hoped that this will serve as an introduction not only to Negro poets and poems, but to all of the worthwhile poetry of the world as well.

Familiarity with the twelve poets included here should be followed by an expanding knowledge of the lives of such poets as Sterling Brown, one of America's eminent men of letters, a poet, author, and teacher, who was born in 1901. He graduated from Williams College in Williamstown, Massachusetts, in 1925, and received his A.M. degree from Harvard University in 1930. He has been professor of English at Howard University, Washington, D.C., since 1929. He was awarded a Guggenheim Fellowship for creative writing in 1938, and is a member of Phi Beta Kappa. His book of poetry, *Southern Road*, was published in 1932; *Negro Poetry and Drama* in 1938, and *The Negro in American Fiction*, in 1938. The two latter volumes are both excellent text books for use in high school and college. Sterling Brown was senior editor of *The Negro Caravan*, 1941, a comprehensive anthology of the writings of American Negroes from the very earliest beginnings. It includes poetry, short stories, essays, and excerpts from biographies, folk literature, as well as drama, personal, social and cultural, and historical essays. He has taught at Lincoln University, in Pennsylvania, Vassar College, Pough-keepsie, New York, Fisk University, in Nashville, Tennessee, and many other universities. At present he is professor of English Literature at Howard University, Washington, D.C.

Georgia Douglas Johnson's works are also well worth knowing. She was born in 1886, and her lyrics are published in several collections which include *The Heart of a Woman*, 1918; *Bronze*, 1922; and *An Autumn Love Cycle*, 1928. More recently, in 1962, she published *Share of My World*. She has contributed to many magazines, including *Vanity Fair*, *Opportunity, a Journal of Negro Life, Crisis*.

The poems of Dr. William E. B. DuBois (1868–1964) are not collected in any one volume of poetry, but are scattered through many periodicals and anthologies of American verse. His poems, along with his scholarly books and essays, are im-portant for every school, home, or public library. It was Dr. DuBois who said of William Stanley Braithwaite in his *Gift of Black Folk*, published by Stratford Company in 1924, "Braithwaite is a critic whose Negro descent is not generally known and has but slightly influenced his work. His place in American literature is due more to his work as a critic and anthologist than to his work as a poet. There is still another role he has played, that of friend of poetry and poets. It is a recognized fact that in the work which preceded the present revival of poetry in the United States, no one rendered more unremitting and valuable service than Mr. Braithwaite. And it can be said that no future study of American poetry of this age can be made without reference to Braithwaite."

Today, it is still important for Negro children to know

13

more about the historical contributions that have been made by Negroes, and it is equally imperative that non-Negro youth know about these contributions that have been made by Negroes.

Most children and young people enjoy participating in poetry reading, whether it is with words or actions. Presenting poetry to youth groups need not be formal—although it can be. It must be a sincere sharing. Whether the poetry is by John Ciardi or Langston Hughes, traditional or modern, read by Helen Hayes or Gwendolyn Brooks or even by one's own mother at home or a teacher at school, if it is good poetry, read well, it will be enjoyed.

JUPITER HAMMON

[1720(?)–1806(?)]

J UPITER HAMMON was a slave of Mr. Henry Lloyd, who lived in Queens Village, Long Island. The dates of his birth and death are not known for certain. The earliest reference to him was found in a letter dated May 19, 1730, when he was perhaps no more than ten years old.

Jupiter Hammon was much respected as a slave preacher and given many special privileges. It is not known when or where he learned to read and write, but his slavery poems were widely circulated. He is the first American Negro poet of whom any known record exists.

His first published work, sometimes referred to as "the first literary effort by any Negro in the United States," was *An Evening Thought: Salvation by Christ, with Penitential Cries,* which appeared as a broadside in 1760. The caption placed on this poem was: "Composed by Jupiter Hammon, a Negro belonging to Mr. Lloyd of Queens Village, on Long Island, the 25th of December, 1760."

It was during this period that Phillis Wheatley became known as a slave poet, also, but Hammon's first poem preceded any by Phillis Wheatley by nine years. His next known work was written for her, and appeared in 1778, eighteen

15

years after his first verse. It is entitled *A Poetical Address to Phillis Wheatley, Ethiopian Poetess,* from which the following stanza is taken:

"While thousands muse with earthly toys,
    And range about the street,
Dear Phillis, seek the heaven's joys,
    Where we do hope to meet."

Hammon next wrote *An Essay on the Ten Virgins,* which was printed in 1779. In 1782, he wrote *A Winter's Piece,* including "A Poem for Children with Thoughts on Death," "An Evening's Improvement," and a rhymed dialogue entitled "The Kind Master and the Dutiful Servant."

A stanza from the poem he wrote especially for children reads:

'Tis God alone can make you wise,
    His wisdom's from above,
He fills the soul with sweet supplies
    By His redeeming love.

From "The Kind Master and the Dutiful Servant," part of the dialogue is as follows:

MASTER

Then will the happy day appear
    That virtue shall increase;
Lay up the sword and drop the spear,
    And nations seek for peace.

SERVANT

Then shall we see the happy end,
Tho' still in some distress;
That distant foes shall act like friends,
And leave their wickedness.

Hammon's most substantial literary work, *An Address to Negroes in the State of New York*, was published in 1787. This book went into three editions.

Hammon's death date is not known, but it is said that he did not die before 1806.

PHILLIS WHEATLEY

[About 1753–1784]

I<small>T WILL</small> be hard for young people to believe that one of America's earliest poets was brought there as a slave child in chains. No one knows exactly when Phillis was born free in Africa, during the latter part of the eighteenth century. Just as hundreds of slaves were kidnapped from their homes, Phillis was stolen and brought to Boston at the age of eight or nine years.

Standing on an auction block with only a piece of old carpet tied around her, she attracted the attention of John Wheatley, a well-to-do tailor. He felt so sorry for the little girl, he immediately bought her as a servant for his invalid wife, and as a companion for his twin children, Mary and Nathaniel.

The entire Wheatley family was captivated by the forlorn little girl. She was treated with great kindness. They called her Phillis, and gave her the family name, Wheatley. She enjoyed a room of her own. Mary had no sister, so she was especially drawn to the little slave child and began at once to teach her to read and write.

Phillis was an apt pupil, and soon learned all that Mary

could teach her. It was the custom at that time for all students to study Latin as well as English, so Mary began teaching Phillis Latin, also. Within sixteen months after her arrival, Phillis was reading the Bible with ease. She soon acquired a knowledge of the elementary sciences, as well.

Phillis was encouraged to write original verses as well as read widely the classics of her day, including Milton, Dryden and Alexander Pope. At the age of fourteen, she began to compose poems to fit certain occasions. A birth, a death, a wedding, or any newsworthy event gave her the opportunity and incentive to write a poem for the event. For six years she wrote avidly about any and all subjects. Her very first publication appeared in 1770, *A Poem by Phillis, a Negro Girl in Boston on the Death of the Reverend George Whitfield*. This was addressed to the Countess of Huntingdon, who was the Reverend Whitfield's patroness. She later befriended Phillis.

Because she was not a strong, healthy girl, Phillis was never given hard work or permitted to be a drudge. She was received in the homes of many of the Wheatleys' friends, and joined the fashionable Old South Church of Boston, a very special privilege for a slave.

When the Revolutionary War broke out, she wrote a poem for General George Washington, and sent it to his headquarters. It appears certain that Phillis Wheatley was the first person to apply to George Washington the phrase 'First in Peace.' The phrase occurs in her poem addressed to His Excellency George Washington, written in 1775. It was used in the resolutions presented to Congress on the death of Washington, December 1799. The closing lines of the poem are:

> Proceed, great chief, with virtue on thy side,
> Thy every action let the goddess guide.

A crown, a mansion, and a throne that shine,
With gold unfading, Washington! be thine.

The General sent her a warm letter of thanks from his encampment and invited her to visit him at his headquarters. The letter read in part: "If you should ever come to Cambridge or near Headquarters, I shall be happy to see a person so favored by the muses, and to whom Nature has been so liberal and beneficient in her dispensations. I am with great respect, Your Obedient Humble Servant, George Washington."

When the Revolutionary War was ended and America had achieved its freedom, Phillis wrote a poem, *Liberty and Peace* which begins:

Lo freedom comes. Th' prescient muse foretold
All eyes th' accomplish'd prophecy behold;
Her port describ'd, "She moves divinely fair,
Olive and laurel bind her golden hair!"

The Wheatley's granted their beloved slave her freedom in 1772, and when she was about twenty years old, she was given a sea voyage because of her delicate health. She went to England as a guest of the Countess Huntingdon, and while she was in London, friends there arranged to have some of her poems published. Her first book, *Poems on Various Subjects, Religious and Moral*, was published in 1773.

The Countess and other friends arranged for her to meet the King, but before this happened, Phillis received word that Mrs. Wheatley was gravely ill, and prepared to leave for America at once. Before she sailed, the Lord Mayor of London presented her with a fine first edition of the great classic, Milton's *Paradise Lost*.

When Phillis arrived back home, Mrs. Wheatley was very ill. She died soon afterwards.

Phillis was sad and lonely following the death of Mrs. Wheatley, as the twins were married and Mr. Wheatley died soon after his wife. Before long, Phillis married a man named John Peters who was a shiftless individual. Three children were born to them, but two of them died in infancy. John Peters left his wife and baby, and Phillis tried to work and take care of herself and the one child that was left. The only work obtainable for her at that time was the hard drudgery of a common boardinghouse. She was not prepared for this kind of life and did not live long. She and her baby died in December, 1784, a little before Christmas, and were buried together.

Phillis Wheatley's poetry must not be judged by the standards of poetry writing today, but by the work and standards of her own day and her own contemporaries. By this method of criticism, she stands out as one of the important personalities in the making of American literature, without any allowances for her sex or her antecedents.

FRANCES ELLEN WATKINS HARPER

[1825–1911]

FRANCES ELLEN WATKINS was born free in Baltimore, Maryland, in 1825. She was a very lonely little girl. Her parents died when she was quite young, and she went to live with an aunt who cared for her until she was old enough to go to the school for free Negro children which was taught by her uncle, the Reverend William Watkins.

Frances attended this school until she was thirteen years old, then began working as a domestic in the homes of well-to-do families. She was quiet and soft-spoken, and learned quickly how to cook, sew, and look after children, easily absorbing all the knowledge she read in the few books that were available in the homes where she worked. Deeply religious, Frances attended church regularly and taught Sunday school, as soon as she was given an opportunity.

Particularly fond of poetry, Frances soon began making verses of her own. Some of her poems found their way into the local newspapers, and there were readers who wondered who the young author could be, as they were convinced that the writing was the work of an unusual person.

In 1850, when Frances was in her mid-twenties and quite

able to take care of herself, she decided to live in a free State, so she moved to Ohio. Because of her excellent training in cooking, sewing, and other household duties, she was asked to teach Domestic Science in a small Negro seminary in Columbus, Ohio. From there she went to Little York, Pennslyvania, where she became acquainted with the accomplishments of the Underground Railroad.

After seeing many slaves rescued and sent on to safety in Canada, Frances joined the antislavery crusade and began taking an active part in the work of this society by writing letters to the press.

In 1853, Maryland enacted a law forbidding free people of color from the North to enter that state. If they did so, they would be imprisoned and sold into slavery. Frances knew first-hand of a free man who unwittingly had violated this infamous statute. He was sold into Georgia, but had escaped by secreting himself behind the wheelhouse of a boat bound northward. Before he reached the desired haven, he was discovered and remanded to slavery. It was reported that he died soon afterwards from the effects of exposure and suffering.

Referring to this outrage, Frances wrote "upon that grave I pledged myself to the Anti-Slavery cause. It may be that God Himself has written upon both my heart and brain a commission to use time, talent, and energy in the cause of freedom."

In her poem, *The Slave Auction*, she reveals with deep feeling the plight of the persons being sold into slavery.

> The sale began—young girls were there,
>   Defenceless in their wretchedness,
> Whose stifled sobs of deep despair
>   Revealed their anguish and distress.

23

And mothers stood with streaming eyes
   And saw their dearest children sold;
Unheeded rose their bitter cries,
   While tyrants bartered them for gold.

And woman, with her love and truth—
   For these in sable forms may dwell—
Gaz'd on the husband of her youth,
   With anguish none may paint or tell.

And men, whose sole crime was their hue,
   The impress of their Maker's hand,
And frail and shrinking children, too,
   Were gathered in that mournful band.

Ye who have laid your love to rest,
   And wept above their lifeless clay,
Know not the anguish of that breast,
   Whose lov'd are rudely torn away.

Ye may not know how desolate
   Are bosoms rudely forced to part,
And how a dull and heavy weight
   Will press the life-drops from the heart.

Frances Ellen Watkins began traveling as a lecturer for the Anti-Slavery Society of Maine on September 28, 1854. She was so successful as a speaker that no door was closed to her. For two years she journeyed through the Eastern states, speaking in churches and to women's clubs, and other anti-slavery groups, until her health failed and she was urged to return to her home in Ohio. In answer to this, she wrote one of her most famous poems, *Bury Me in a Free Land*.

Make me a grave where'er you will,
In a lowly plain, or a lofty hill;
Make it among earth's humblest graves
But not in a land where men are slaves.

I could not rest if around my grave
I heard the steps of a trembling slave;
His shadow above my silent tomb
Would make it a place of fearful gloom.

I could not rest if I heard the tread
Of a coffle gang to the shambles led,
And the mother's shriek of wild despair
Rise like a curse on the trembling air.

I could not sleep if I saw the lash
Drinking her blood at each fearful gash,
And I saw her babes torn from her breast,
Like trembling doves from their parent nest.

I'd shudder and start if I heard the bay
Of bloodhounds seizing their human prey,
And I heard the captive plead in vain
As they bound afresh his galling chain.

If I saw young girls from their mother's arms
Bartered and sold for their youthful charms,
My eye would flash with a mournful flame,
My death-paled cheek grow red with shame.

I would sleep, dear friends, where bloated might
Can rob no man of his dearest right;
My rest shall be calm in any grave
Where none can call his brother a slave.

I ask no monument, proud and high,
To arrest the gaze of the passers-by;
All that my yearning spirit craves,
Is bury me not in a land of slaves.

In 1860, Frances Ellen Watkins married Fenton Harper, in Cincinnati, Ohio. She gave up traveling, but continued to write for antislavery journals. Following the death of her husband, on May 23, 1864, just before the close of the Civil War, she began writing in earnest, and also went back to the lecture platform.

When the War between the States was ended, Frances traveled through the South, talking to the newly-freed men and women in an effort to encourage them. "Now is the time," she said, "for our women to begin to lift up their heads and plant the roots of progress under the hearthstone."

Simultaneously, she began to devote a good part of her time to the work of the Women's Christian Temperance Union. At the World's Meeting of that organization, held in Philadelphia in November, 1922, Frances Harper was given one of their highest honors. Her name was placed on the *Red Letter* Calendar, beside those of Frances E. Willard, Lady Henry Somerset, and other great supporters of temperance.

Her published works include both poetry and prose. She was the first Negro woman to have a full-length novel published. It was titled *Iola Leroy-The Shadows Uplifted*, and appeared in 1860, the year of her marriage. Her first volume of poetry, *Poems on Miscellaneous Subjects*, was issued in 1854. Others are, *Poems* (1871); *Sketches of Southern Life* (1872); *The Slave Auction*; and *Bury Me in a Free Land*.

Frances Ellen Watkins Harper died on February 22, 1911. Her slim volumes of social protest are now treasured as collector's items.

JAMES WELDON JOHNSON

[1871-1938]

JAMES WELDON JOHNSON was born in Jacksonville, Florida, on June 17, 1871, the second child of his parents, James and Helen Louise Johnson. A little sister, born in Nassau, where the family lived previously, had died earlier.

James Johnson, the father, was headwaiter in a big tourist hotel. He was thrifty and soon built a new home for his family in Jacksonville. There a second boy, John Rosamond, who became almost as famous as James Weldon, was born in August of 1873.

When they were small boys, both sons enjoyed visiting their father at the hotel, where the waiters who worked for him made a big fuss over them. Their father made kites and boats for them, and took them on jolly picnicking trips. Their mother loved books, and often read aloud to young James and John Rosamond. The boys were fascinated by the adventures of *David Copperfield*, and *Robert the Bruce, King of Scotland*, and their father introduced them to Shakespeare and Plutarch. Their favorite books, however, were *Pickwick Papers* and the *Waverly Novels*.

James Weldon, particularly, liked the *Fairy Tales* of the Grimm Brothers and the beautiful stories of Hans Christian

Andersen. Best of all, he liked the story of the "Chinese Nightingale." This led him later to a love of John Keats' poetry, especially his "Ode to the Nightingale," because it, too, gave him a sense of beauty and a longing for the truth found in beautiful things.

Mrs. Johnson was her sons' first music teacher, as well as their first schoolteacher. From the time they were small, the boys would stand at each end of the keyboard of their household organ and sing. Their mother would play the hymn tunes, while their father accompanied them on his guitar.

She also taught the boys to read, as she was a teacher in the grade school for Negro children in Jacksonville. In later life, James Weldon recalled vaguely how crowded and uncomfortable this school was. Their father soon found a better school for them. It was called Stanton, and was an excellent grammar school for Negroes. Here young James promptly fell in love with his teacher, Miss Carrie Sampson. He said she was one of the loveliest women he had ever seen, and he wept when he was promoted and had to leave her class.

Soon after James Weldon finished grammar school, his father entered him in Atlanta University—for there was no high school for Negro children in all of Florida. The brilliant boy was well prepared for higher education. He attended Atlanta with a foster brother, Ricardo Rodrigues Ponce, a young Spanish-speaking Cuban, who made his home with the Johnsons and became practically a third son in the household. James and John soon learned to speak fluent Spanish from this companion, and since their father spoke both languages as headwaiter in the tourist hotel, it was a bi-lingual family. James' knowledge of Spanish was to deeply affect his life in later years, for he served his country well in Latin America, and he translated many beautiful poems of these Spanish-speaking peoples into English.

To earn his way through the University, James Weldon taught summers in rural Negro schools of Georgia. He was paid the pitiful sum of five cents a day for each child taught— yet this was enough to take care of his tuition. In 1894, after graduation from Atlanta, he returned to Stanton, his old school, as its principal. He soon saw that Negro boys and girls must have a high-school education to become teachers and professional men and women, so he made Stanton into a high school. It was at Stanton that he and his brother J. Rosamond, now an accomplished musician and composer, wrote "Lift Every Voice and Sing," in honor of Lincoln's birthday. Within a few years, this became known as the Negro National Hymn. Its melody is as distinguished as its words:

Sing a song full of the faith that the dark past has taught us,
Sing a song full of the hope that the present has brought us,
Facing the rising sun of our new day begun
Let us march on till victory is won.

During the time that Johnson was principal of Stanton, he was editor of the first Negro daily paper in the United States, *The Daily American.* And he also began the study of law in the approved manner of the South, by reading law in the office of a brilliant young member of the Jacksonville bar, Thomas A. Ledwith. Within six months he was Ledwith's assistant in drawing up bills in divorce cases, and at the end of eighteen months he was told by Ledwith that "he felt he was ready for the bar examinations." Johnson was the first Negro in Florida to appear before its three-member examining board, for admittance to the bar. The three men, all white, had made up their minds not to admit a Negro. They asked more and more difficult questions, even very intricate questions about international law. When young James Weldon had answered every one of them correctly, in spite of the obstacles placed in his way, they sent him out of the room. One of the Board members declared that he would never be a party to admitting a Negro man to the Bar; the other men were more fair-minded. They saw that the candidate had passed extraordinarily well, so they voted two to one to admit him.

All young lawyers have a difficult time getting business after they "hang out their shingles," waiting for clients and proving themselves in the courtroom, but it was particularly difficult for a young Negro in an all-white profession. The people of his own race needed lawyers frequently, but most of them were wretchedly poor and racial predjudice made it practically impossible for them to win cases in a Southern court, especially with a Negro lawyer as council.

"What's the use of being a lawyer where there is no real justice?" Johnson asked himself, and finally, after much discouragement and many disheartening experiences, he gave up his legal profession and went to New York. His brother, J. Rosamond, went with him. They had lived previously for several summers with a great aunt in Brooklyn, so were quite familiar with Manhattan, which they had often visited with their uncle. The two brothers took with them a comic opera they had written and composed together. They could find no one to produce it, but a successful young Negro singer, Bob Cole, was delighted with the comic words and gay tunes.

Cole offered to collaborate with the Johnsons, and while they were working on their songs, they met almost everyone of any importance in the musical comedy field in New York—

Reginald de Koven and Isadore Witmark, owner of a music publishing firm; Bert Williams, great Negro comic, and his partner, George Walker; Will Marion Cook, composer, and Harry T. Burleigh, singer and musician, great Negro performers. Even the famous conductor of the New York Philharmonic, Oscar Hammerstein, climbed the four flights of stairs to the top of the house on West 53rd Street where the Johnsons lived, to hear them play and sing their satiric and comic songs.

Paul Laurence Dunbar, most successful of Negro poets in that time, came to New York for the production of *Clorindy—The Origin of the Cakewalk*, which he had written in collaboration with Will Marion Cook. The Johnsons met him at a rehearsal, and he, too, frequently visited them at their apartment, the central meeting place for some of the brightest lights of the New York stage. Their friendship was very close until Dunbar's death only a few years later.

From 1901 to 1906, James Weldon spent his winters teaching at Stanton, while J. Rosamond continued with his private music instruction for the young people of Jacksonville. In the summers, the brothers went north, to New York, where, during those five years, they published a number of song hits, among them *Under the Bamboo Tree, Li'l Gal, Maiden with the Dreamy Eyes, Since You Went Away*, and many others that are still popular.

Theodore Roosevelt was President of the United States during this time, having taken office following the assassination of President McKinley. When he ran for his second term, the Johnson brothers wrote his campaign song. It was after what James Weldon called "his glorious victory," that the President came to know the song writer, but in quite a different way. President Roosevelt was always interested in the literary

DR. W. E. B. DUBOIS

Courtesy Museum of Negro History and Art

PHILLIS WHEATLEY

By permission of The Associated Publishers, Inc.

JAMES WELDON
JOHNSON

FRANCES ELLEN
WATKINS HARPER

PAUL LAURENCE
DUNBAR

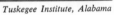

Tuskegee Institute, Alabama

EFFIE LEE
NEWSOME

ARNA BONTEMPS

LANGSTON HUGHES

Courtesy Museum of Negro History and Art

COUNTEE CULLEN

MARGARET WALKER

GWENDOLYN BROOKS

figures of his day, and it was through Brander Matthews, teacher of literature and drama specialist, that James Weldon was invited to the White House. James had been a pupil of Matthews, continuing his academic study, as he did all his life.

In order to give James more time for his writing, the President appointed him Consul to Puerto Cabello, in Venezuela. Johnson, who spoke fluent Spanish, was so successful in this assignment that the State Department moved him to a more difficult post—at Corinto, in Nicaragua, a troubled land where revolutions were constantly threatening or taking place. Johnson served as consul through three revolutions. The Americans living there could not help but admire their cool-headed, courteous, always hospitable representative and his courage in protecting their lives and property.

While on a leave of absence in New York, James fell in love with and married Grace Nail, whom he had known from her girlhood. He brought her back to Corinto, where she served as a lovely hostess in the consulate. She quickly learned to speak colloquial and vivid Spanish, from having to deal with the servants and tradespeople. It was something of an ordeal for the bride from Brooklyn, but she made their home attractive with grass green rugs and wicker furniture, and was a delightful companion for the consul.

Two sorrows came to James Weldon Johnson while he was out of the States. First, his old friend and collaborator, Bob Cole, died. Soon after that, his father, who had exerted such a lasting influence on the lives of both sons, died also.

While still serving as consul, James Weldon was constantly publishing articles on Negro and minority problems, especially as they affected the relations between the United States and Latin America. He had also begun to write very serious and beautiful poetry, quite different from the light lyrics of his popular song years. On the 50th Anniversary of the signing of the Emancipation Proclamation, he wrote "Fifty Years— 1863-1913," which presents a review of the Negro's contribution to America.

> O brothers mine, today we stand
> Where half a century sweeps our ken
> Since God, through Lincoln's ready hand,
> Struck off our bonds and made us men.

Many other fine verses are included in this poem, which may be read in the anthology, *Fifty-Years and Other Poems*, published in 1917.

As Johnson was writing his articles and poems, he was also working on his full-length novel, *The Autobiography of an Ex-Colored Man*. Many persons have thought it was the story of the author's own life, and so, to refute this impression, many years later, in 1933, he published, through the Viking Press in New York, and Macmillan Company of Canada, Ltd., *Along This Way*, the real account of his life. This, as it reviews the events of the years between 1871 and 1933, is considered by many to be among the greatest autobiographies of an American written in this century.

Even after Johnson "retired" to private life, and the administration at Washington had changed, his interests continued to be rich and varied. He became Field Secretary for the National Association for the Advancement of Colored People, and during the next fourteen years, from 1916 to 1930, entered more fully than he had previously into the redressing of the wrongs done his race. He fought long and diligently, with his whole heart and soul, to persuade Congress to pass an antilynching law. While the Senate was debating the bill, on May 6, 1921, a mob at Kirbin, Texas, burned three Negroes alive, one after another! The bill, however, was never passed.

For a long time, Johnson had felt that in the Negro folk songs and spirituals, and the poetic utterances of the old-time preachers, there lay a wealth of material for poets and composers of music to draw upon for inspiration. In his *O Black and Unknown Bards*, he wrote:

> O black and unknown bards of long ago,
> How came your lips to touch the sacred fire?
> How, in your darkness, did you come to know
> The power and beauty of the minstrel's lyre?

He decided to turn the traditional and splendid sermons, delivered by Methodist and Baptist preachers of his boyhood, into poems. Deeply influenced by Walt Whitman's *Leaves of Grass*, he did a most remarkable recreation of these Negro preacher's inspired and poetic speech in *God's Trombones, Seven Negro Sermons in Verse*. Among his favorite "sermons" were The Creation, The Building of the Ark, The Escape of the Egyptian slaves under their leader, Moses, and four other well-known incidents from the Bible. These he turned into splendid poems.

In the old meetings in the churches, the opening prayer was frequently given by a woman, and Johnson introduces his book with such a prayer, or invocation, in these words:

> O Lord, we come this morning
> Knee-bowed and body-bent
> Before Thy throne of grace.
> We come this morning—

Like empty pitchers to a full fountain,
With no merits of our own.
O Lord—open up a window of heaven,
And lean out far over the battlements of glory,
And listen this morning.

Other outstanding works of James Weldon Johnson are, his anthology, *The Book of American Negro Poetry* (1922) and a later edition, (1931), and *Saint Peter Relates an Incident of the Resurrection Day* (1930). The latter, with wit and irony, describes the prejudices of the American people. One of our best literary critics said of this long poem, "In it we find Johnson's most deeply moving qualities: understanding, imagination, sincerity, and poise." It is his most mature work. With his brother, J. Rosamond, he gathered and edited and not only harmonized but wrote a magnificent introduction for *The Book of American Negro Spirituals* (1925) and *The Second Book of American Negro Spirituals* (1926). The introduction gives insight into the cultural background of the Africans who came to the Americas, and is a fine contribution to the nation's understanding of the race.

When he was in his sixties, James Weldon still remained active in literary circles and in teaching. He was an instructor at Fisk University, in Nashville, Tennessee, which awarded him an honorary degree of Doctor of Laws, and established for him the Adam K. Spence Chair of Creative Literature. He became a profound influence in the lives of the younger Negro poets and scholars during the 1930's, and might have gathered around him many literary disciples if it had not been for his tragic and sudden death.

In his Funeral Sermon in Verse, "Go Down Death," in *God's Trombones*, he wrote his own elegy:

And God sat back on his throne,
And he commanded that tall, bright Angel standing at
    his right hand:
Call me death!
And that tall, bright angel cried in a voice
That broke like a clap of thunder:

Call Death!—Call Death!
And the echo sounded down the streets of heaven
Till it reached away back in that shadowy place,
Where death waits with his pale, white horses.

In the summer of 1938, while driving in his car near his summer cottage in Maine, James Weldon Johnson was struck and killed by a train at a railroad crossing. America lost a great civil servant, the Negro people, a great leader, and all the world, a prophetic voice that still speaks out loud and clear to us today.

PAUL LAURENCE DUNBAR

[1872–1906]

PAUL LAURENCE DUNBAR was born in Dayton, Ohio, on June 27, 1872. His mother, Matilda Murphy, was reared as a slave on a plantation near Shelbyville, Kentucky. Her master and mistress were Kentuckians of culture. Theirs was a home filled with books and people who read widely. Matilda was very witty and had an amazing memory, so that years later, she was able to tell many stories about her life on the plantation. These stories were used as a background for much of the poetry of her son, Paul, as well as in his other writing.

While still a slave, Matilda married R. Weeks Murphy. Two sons were born to them, Willam T. and Robert S. Murphy. When her husband died, she moved with her two small boys to Dayton, Ohio, and there tried to make a living by doing laundry work. She met and married Joshua Dunbar, who had been a soldier in the War between the States.

When her third son was born, there was a great deal of discussion about what his name should be. The father, who was much the senior of his wife, was sometimes considered old-fashioned. He suggested a name from the Bible. "This child," he said, "will be great some day, and do you honor. The Bible says Paul was a great man." And so they named their baby Paul for the prophet and Laurence as a compliment to a family friend.

Paul loved to hear his father talk about his life in the Army, particularly about his own regiment, the famous Fifty-Fourth, and the attack on Fort Wagner. But he also never tired of hearing his mother tell about her life on the plantation. She had a real gift for recreating the scenes of her childhood for him. She had taught herself to read by picking up a word here and there, often watching her children at their homework. For a short time she was able to attend a night school, but trying to help provide even a sparse living for the family by washing and ironing was hard, and she was much too tired at night to study. However, she was never too tired to answer the questions of her youngest son.

When Paul was about four years of age, his mother began teaching him his letters and soon thereafter he began to scribble verses. His first "poetical achievement" was reciting some of his own poems at the Easter exercises of his Sunday School.

Joshua Dunbar died in a home for old soldiers when Paul was twelve years old, and his two half-brothers went away to Chicago, in order to find work. This left Paul and his mother alone. She took in washing for the well-to-do families and the boy delivered the heavy baskets of clean clothes.

He was a serious student and soon entered Central High School where he was well liked by his teachers and classmates. Among his best friends were the two sons of a minister, the Wright brothers, Orville and Wilbur, of airplane fame. They and their younger sister were motherless, but the boys were devoted to her and took excellent care of her. Paul was treated as one of the Wright family, and was allowed to help the boys with their paper, which they printed by hand. He not only delivered it, but was also invited to contribute a poem now and then. He wrote this one to help promote sales:

> Come, come assist me truant muse!
> For I would sing of the West Side News.
> A sheet that's newsy, pure, and bright—
> Whose editor is Orville Wright,
> And by his side another shines
> Whom you shall know as Edwin Sines.
> Now all will buy this sheet, I trust,
> And watch out for their April bust.

When Paul Dunbar graduated from Central High School in Cleveland, in June, 1891, he had served as editor of the high school paper. His Dutch music teacher had said, "Mr. Dunbar, you have no music in your soul," but the words he submitted for the Class Song won for him the honor of being selected Class Poet. It goes

> Why stirs with sad alarm, the heart,
> For all who meet must some day part?
> So, let no useless cavil be;
> True wisdom bows to God's decree.
>
> The wind is fair, the sails are spread,
> Let hearts be firm. "Godspeed" is said.
> Before us lies the untried way
> And we're impatient at the stay.
>
> At last we move; how thrills the heart,
> So long impatient for the start!
> Now up o'er hill and down through dell
> The echoes bring our song—farewell!

While he was still in high school, Paul found a job as elevator boy in the Callahan Building on Main Street in Dayton, Ohio. He received four dollars a week for his services! As he went up and down in his elevator, he wrote verses and little sketches, and sent them out to magazines, but they were promptly returned. He was not discouraged, however. One happy day, the Rochester, New York, *Herald* accepted his "Christmas Is A-Comin'," and it was published December 24, 1891. A few other poems were purchased by newspapers.

The Western Writers' Association met in Dayton, in 1892, and one of his former teachers, Mrs. Helen M. Truesdell, persuaded the group to invite young Paul Dunbar to make the welcoming address. He asked permission to leave his elevator long enough to deliver his short speech. The program was held on his twentieth birthday and he was thrilled to have it the occasion of his first major address.

He walked down the aisle of the auditorium with dignity, mounted the platform and recited:

"Westward the course of empire takes its way,
  So Berkeley said, and so today
  The men who know the world still say.
  The glowing West, with bounteous hand,
  Bestows her gifts throughout the land,
  And smiles to see at her command
  Art, science, and the industries,
  New fruits of new Hesperides.
  So proud are you who claim the West
  As home land; doubly are you blest
  To live where liberty and health
  Go hand in hand with brains and wealth.
  So here's a welcome to you all,

Whate'er the work your hands let fall,
To you who trace on history's page
The footprints of each passing age;
To you who tune the laureled lyre
To songs of love or deeds of fire;
To you before whose well-wrought tale
The cheek doth flush or brow grow pale;
To you who bow the ready knee
And worship cold philosophy,
A welcome warm as Western wine,
And free as Western hearts, be thine.
Do what the greatest joy insures,
The city has no will but yours."

He bowed and promptly departed from the auditorium, leaving a thrilled audience behind him. Two of the most prominent members were sent to find the young poet. They were Dr. James Newton Matthews and Mr. Will Pfrimmer. They discovered him in his elevator, waiting to take the patrons to their floors. On his little stool were his pencil, a "tablet" (pad of paper) and *The Century Magazine*, which he read constantly. His greatest ambition was to have a poem published in this magazine!

Paul tried to talk with his two visitors while listening for the elevator bell to ring as he continued to carry his passengers up and down. The two men questioned him about his life and asked to see more of his poems.

An article about the meeting of the Western Writers' Association and the welcoming address given by young Paul, appeared in the daily paper. This was read by James Whitcomb Riley, the famous Midwestern poet, who wrote to Paul on November 27, 1892, and wished him "every good thing."

Dunbar prized this letter highly and immediately composed a poem for Riley. These lines are included in Paul Laurence Dunbar's first collection of poetry and later were reprinted in his *Complete Poems*. He also wrote a poem on the death of John Greenleaf Whittier, in September 1892.

Paul began to think about trying to have a book of his poems published. His mother had kept all of them, carefully tucking away in a box under the bed every scrap of paper on which he had written a verse. Some friends of his encouraged him by promises to see about getting them published, but nothing came of this.

Finally, in 1895, Paul went to the publishing house of the United Brethren, a religious concern. A representative of the firm informed him that the poems could not be published on a regular royalty basis and, in fact, that their company could not assume the responsibility unless the author paid one hundred and twenty-five dollars. Paul asked if they would print the book and permit him to pay later, but the answer was, "No, not unless there is ample security."

Paul Dunbar had no money nor did he have any security. Discouraged, he had turned to leave when Mr. William Blacher, the business manager of the company, glanced up and saw how dejected he looked. Feeling sorry for him, he asked what he could do. Paul explained that the firm would not trust him for one hundred and twenty-five dollars so that he could have his verses printed. The business manager felt so sorry for the downcast young poet he offered to give his personal guarantee for the book and assured him it could be published in time for the Christmas holidays.

Although Paul had graduated from high school nearly two years earlier, he was well remembered by many of his former classmates. When they heard about his publishing problems, they pledged their support, along with several of his other friends. On a snowy day just before Christmas, the postman brought a large package to the Dunbar home addressed to Mr. Paul Dunbar. It contained a number of copies of his printed book of poems, called *Oak and Ivy*.

Paul sold the book to the elevator passengers where he worked and to the students from his high school for one dollar each, and within two weeks after publication, he was back at the publishing house with one hundred and twenty-five dollars, the full amount of his obligation. All the books were sold!

Dr. H. A. Tobey of Toledo, Ohio, was one of Dunbar's most loyal supporters and a devoted friend. He had introduced Paul to some of the people who bought his book, so the author dedicated this first book of poems, *Oak and Ivy*, to Dr. H. A. Tobey, "To my friend who aided me financially in the publication of my first book."

Soon after this, Paul began to look for a better job than that of elevator man. He traveled to Chicago, where the Columbian Exposition, a great World's Fair, was being held. There he met Frederick Douglass, the famous Negro orator and liberator, who had charge of the Exhibit from Haiti. Douglass gave Paul a job at five dollars a week as one of his assistants. The Fair featured "days" honoring various groups and on Colored American Day both Dunbar and Douglass appeared on the same platform.

Paul was soon in demand as a reader of his poems. He was invited to appear on Negro college campuses throughout the South. He later went to Washington, D.C., where Frederick Douglass helped him get a job as a clerk in the Library of Congress.

Two volumes of his poetry were published in 1896. *Majors*

and Minors, the second book, was privately printed and William Dean Howells wrote an enthusiastic review, which appeared in *Harper's Weekly* for June 27, 1896, Paul's birthday. The same issue of the magazine announced the nomination of William McKinley for the Presidency, so tens of thousands of extra copies were printed. This spread the news of the young poet, not only throughout the country, but to foreign lands as well.

Among the new poems included in *Majors and Minors* was the beautiful *The Poet and His song*, and the much loved *Ere Sleep Comes Down to Soothe the Weary Eyes*.

ERE SLEEP COMES DOWN TO SOOTHE THE WEARY EYES

Ere sleep comes down to soothe the weary eyes,
   Which all the day with ceaseless care have sought
The magic gold which from the seeker flies;
   Ere dreams put on the gown and cap of thought,
And make the waking world a world of lies,—
   Of lies most palpable, uncouth, forlorn,
That say life's full of aches and tears and sight,—
   Oh, how with more than dreams the soul is torn,
Ere sleep comes down to soothe the weary eyes.

Ere sleep comes down to soothe the weary eyes,
   How all the griefs and heartaches we have known
Come up like pois'nous vapors that arise
   From some base witch's caldron, when the crone,
To work some potent spell, her magic plies.
   The past which held its share of bitter pain,
Whose ghost we prayed that Time might exorcise,

Comes up, is lived and suffered o'er again,
Ere sleep comes down to soothe the weary eyes.

Ere sleep comes down to soothe the weary eyes,
   What phantoms fill the dimly lighted room;
What ghostly shades in awe-creating guise
   Are bodied forth within the teeming gloom.
What echoes faint of sad and soul-sick cries,
   And pangs of vague inexplicable pain
That pay the spirit's ceaseless enterprise,
   Come thronging through the chambers of the brain,
Ere sleep comes down to soothe the weary eyes.

Ere sleep comes down to soothe the weary eyes,
   Where ranges forth the spirit far and free?
Through what strange realms and unfamiliar skies
   Tends her far course to lands of mystery?
To lands unspeakable—beyond surmise,
   Where shapes unknowable to being spring,
Till, faint of wing, the Fancy fails and dies
   Much wearied with the spirit's journeying,
Ere sleep comes down to soothe the weary eyes.

Ere sleep comes down to soothe the weary eyes,
   How questioneth the soul that other soul,
The inner sense which neither cheats nor lies,
   But self exposes unto self, a scroll
Full writ with all life's acts unwise or wise,
   In characters indelible and known;
So, trembling with the shock of sad surprise,
   The soul doth view its awful self alone,
Ere sleep comes down to soothe the weary eyes.

When sleep comes down to seal the weary eyes,
  The last dear sleep whose soft embrace is balm,
And whom sad sorrow teaches us to prize
  For kissing all our passions into calm,
Ah, then, no more we heed the sad world's cries,
  Or seek to probe th' eternal mystery,
Or fret our souls at long-withheld replies,
  At glooms through which our visions cannot see,
When sleep comes down to seal the weary eyes.

In the same year, 1896, Dodd, Mead and Company was the first regular trade publishing firm to accept Paul Dunbar's works. They published *Lyrics of Lowly Life* and the *Century Magazine asked* for two of his poems! The book was dedicated "To My Mother" and William Dean Howells wrote the introduction.

The following year, Paul went to London for Queen Victoria's Diamond Jubilee, where he read his poems to large audiences. He received hundreds of letters and telegrams and messages of congratulation. Among these was a letter written by a young lady from New Orleans, Louisiana, Alice Ruth Moore, who was also a poet. Paul met her when he returned from London. They fell in love with each other and were married on March 6, 1898, in New York City. The couple were extremely happy for a short while, but Dunbar's health began to fail and their marriage did not last.

Paul resigned from the Library of Congress, but he continued to lecture and to write. Booker T. Washington invited him to Tuskegee, Alabama. Paul Dunbar wrote the Tuskegee song for the twenty-fifth anniversary of the school. He met the distinguished author and poet, James Weldon Johnson, and his brother, J. Rosamond Johnson, the musician, and collaborated with them in writing the lyrics used in eight musical shows. Among these was *Clorinda—Origin of the Cake Walk*, which was performed for an entire theatrical season in New York, during 1898.

Forty of Paul Dunbar's poems were set to music by such famous musicians as Carrie Jacobs Bond, Harry T. Burleigh, Walter Damrosch, J. Rosamond Johnson, Franco Leoni, and the celebrated Samuel Coleridge Taylor of London, England.

Many of Dunbar's poems are beautifully composed, in very literary English, but he is best known for those written in the old-time Negro dialect of the plantation days. A popular and charming poem in dialect children love and enjoy is:

LITTLE BROWN BABY

Little brown baby wif spa'klin' eyes,
   Come to yo' pappy an' set on his knee.
What you been doin', suh—makin' san' pies?
   Look at dat bib—you's ez du'ty ez me.
Look at dat mouf—dat's merlasses, I bet;
   Come hyeah, Maria, an' wipe off his han's.
Bees gwine to ketch you an' eat you yit,
   Bein' so sticky an' sweet—goodness lan's!

Little brown baby wif spa'klin eyes,
   Who's pappy's darlin' and who's pappy's chile?
Who is it all de day nevah once tries
   Fu' to be cross, er once loses dat smile?
Whah did you git dem teef? My, you's a scamp!
   Whah did dat dimple come f'om in yo' chin?
Pappy do' know you—I b'lieves you's a tramp;
   Mammy, dis hyeah's some ol' straggler got in!

Let's th'ow him outen de do' in de san',
　We do' want stragglers a-layin' 'roun' hyeah;
Let's gin him 'way to de big buggah-man;
　I know he's hidin' erroun' hyeah right neah.
Buggah-man, buggah-man, come in de do',
　Hyeah's a bad boy you kin have fu' to eat.
Mammy and pappy do' want him no mo',
　Swaller him down f'om his haid to his feet!

Dah, now, I t'ought dat you'd hug me up close.
　Go back, ol' buggah, you sha'n't have dis boy,
He ain't no tramp, ner no straggler, of co'se;
　He's pappy's pa'dner an' playmate an' joy.
Come to yo' pallet now—go to yo' res';
　Wisht you could allus know ease an' cleah skies;
Wisht you could stay jes' a chile on my breas'—
　Little brown baby wif spa'klin' eyes!

Paul Laurence Dunbar captured the mischief found in most children, especially boys, who are always hungry and want to get right down to the business of eating, in his poem entitled *In The Morning,* which is one of the favorites of all children.

'Lias! 'Lias! Bless de Lawd!
Don' you know de day's erbroad?
Ef you don' git up, you scamp,
Dey'll be trouble in dis camp.
T'ink I gwine to let you sleep
W'ile I meks yo' boa'd an' keep?
Dat's a putty howdy-do—
Don' you hyeah me, 'Lias—you?

Bet ef I come crost dis flo'
You won' fin' no time to sno'.
Daylight all a-shinin' in
W'ile you sleep—w'y his's a sin!
Ain't de can'le-light enough
To bu'n out widout a snuff,
But you go de mo'nin' thoo
Bu'in' up de daylight too?

'Lias, don' you hyeah me call?
No use tu'nin' to'ds de wall;
I kin hyeah dat mattuss squeak;
Don' you hyeah me w'en I speak?
Dis hyeah clock don struck off six—
Ca'line, bring me dem ah sticks!
Oh, you down, suh; huh, you down—
Look hyeah, don' you daih to frown.

Ma'ch yo' se'f an' wash yo' face,
Don' you splattah all de place;
I got somep'n else to do,
'Sides jes' cleanin' aftah you.
Tek dat comb an' fix yo' haid—
Looks jes' lak a feddah baid.
Look hyeah, boy, I let you see
You sha'n't roll yo' eyes at me.

Come heyah; bring me dat ah strap!
Boy, I'll whup you 'twell you drop;
You done felt yo'se'f too strong
An' you sholy got me wrong.
Set down at dat table thaih;

Jes' you whimpah ef you daih!
Evah mo'nin' on dis place
Seem lak I mus' lose my grace.

Fol' yo' han's an' bow yo' haid—
Wait ontwell de blessin' 's said;
"Lawd, have mussy on ouah souls—"
(Don' you daih to tech dem rolls—)
"Bless de food we gwine to eat—"
(You set still—I see yo' feet;)
(You jes' try dat trick again!)
"Gin us peace an' joy. Amen!"

In addition to a large number of poems, Paul Laurence
Dunbar is the author of four novels and several volumes of
short stories. Fifteen of his short stories appeared in such
magazines as *Lippincott's* and *The Saturday Evening Post*.
Forty articles and essays were written for *Harper's Weekly*,
The Century, *Smart Set*, and other periodicals. He was
awarded an honorary degree by Atlanta University.

Dunbar's doctors advised him to go to the Rocky Mountains for his health. In addition to his illness, he was grieving
for his wife and his broken marriage. He died on Lincoln's
birthday, in 1906, and was buried in Dayton, Ohio. He wrote
his own farewell which, fittingly enough, is carved on his
tombstone. It is:

A DEATH SONG

Lay me down beneaf de willers in de grass,
Whah de branch'll go a-singin' as it pass.
An' w'en I's a-layin' low,

I kin hyeah it as it go
Singin', "Sleep, my honey, tek yo' res' at las'."

Lay me nigh to whah hit meks a little pool,
An' de watah stan's so quiet lak an' cool,
   Whah de little birds in spring,
   Ust to come an' drink an' sing,
An' de chillen waded on dey way to school.

Let me settle w'en my shouldahs draps dey load
Nigh enough to hyeah de noises in de road;
   Fu' I t'ink de las' long res'
   Gwine to soothe my sperrit bes'
Ef I's layin' 'mong de t'ings I's allus knowed.

Hundreds of poetry lovers visit Paul Laurence Dunbar's grave each year. His mother planted a willow beside it. There are many living memorials or tributes to his memory, such as a huge housing development in New York City and dozens of Negro schools and college dormitories throughout the United States. There are also Negro banks, insurance firms, and other Negro businesses bearing his name, which will live forever in the hearts of those who love his poetry.

WILLIAM STANLEY
BRAITHWAITE

[1878–1962]

WILLIAM STANLEY BRAITHWAITE was born on December 6, 1878, in Boston, Massachusetts, where the family had settled after migrating from the West Indies. His father, William Smith Braithwaite, was the son of a distinguished colonial family of British Guiana, and his mother, Emma DeWolfe Braithwaite, was the daughter of an ex-slave.

When William Stanley was eight years old, his father died, leaving the family destitute. His mother became a domestic and he had to find work, after only four years of public schooling. Fortunately, he secured a job as a messenger with a publishing firm, Ginn and Company. The messenger boys sat in an outer office, to wait their turns between errands. They often played tricks on each other while waiting, but William Stanley was seldom included in the fun. Instead, he liked to look at the books that lined the shelves of the office. His employer noticed the quiet, shy boy and gave him permission to read while he waited for his errands.

The first book William read was Church's *Greek Gods and Heroes.* After this, he read avidly everything that was on the shelves. One day his employer asked if he would like to

53

learn the trade of a compositor. William was so surprised he hardly knew how to answer! His mother consented for him to become an apprentice, and the foundation for his life's work began.

His first job as a typesetter was working on one of John Keats' poems. This was followed by the verse of William Wordsworth and, later, by some of the lyrics of Robert Burns. Before he realized it, William was composing verses of his own! He began to print these on unused galleys at the end of the day. Nothing that he wrote later gave him quite the thrill that he derived from seeing his own name on those early galley sheets.

Braithwaite's struggles, at the beginning of his career as a writer, were very hard. There were no fellowships available in those days when he embarked upon a literary career. When a publisher offered to bring out his book of verse only at his own expense, he tramped the streets of Boston for months, trying to get subscribers. Some of the persons who helped by agreeing to buy the book were Julia Ward Howe, Thomas Bailey Aldrich, Bliss Perry, Mary A. DeWolfe Howe, and Edward Everett Hale. When it was finally published in 1904, Braithwaite delivered the volumes himself.

This collection of his poetry was called *Lyrics of Life and Love*. It was followed by *The House of Falling Leaves*, in 1908, and *Sandy Star and Willie Gee*, in 1922. Braithwaite's poetry is marked by delicate beauty, often tinged by mysticism or whimsy. He was skilled in the subtleties of poetic effect, and, when he wished, could be a superb lyricist, as shown in his *Rhapsody*.

I am glad daylong for the gift of song,
For time and change and sorrow;

For the sunset wings and the world-end things
Which hang on the edge of tomorrow.
I am glad for my heart whose gates apart
Are the entrance-place of wonders,
Where dreams come in from the rush and din
Like sheep from the rains and thunders.

William Stanley Braithwaite is best known for his anthologies of collected magazine verse by various authors. These started in 1913 and continued until 1929. He was one of the pioneers in stimulating the "revival" of poetry in the United States. Many of the works of America's leading poets first appeared in the Braithwaite publications, before they were included in other anthologies. Edgar Lee Master's *Spoon River* collections, Vachel Lindsay's *Chants*, and Carl Sandburg's free verse are some of the fine poetic writings first collected by Braithwaite.

In 1948, William Stanley Braithwaite was awarded the Spingarn Medal by the National Association for the Advancement of Colored People for "high achievement by an American Negro." He worked on the editorial staff of the *Boston Transcript* for several years, and was professor of Creative Literature at Atlanta University until his retirement in 1945. Honorary degrees were conferred on him by Atlanta University and Taladega College.

EFFIE LEE NEWSOME

[1885–   ]

M ARY EFFIE LEE NEWSOME was born in Philadelphia, Pennsylvania, January 19, 1885. Her father was a minister of the African Methodist Episcopal Church, and she says, "My younger sister, Consuelo, and I, lived in a narrow red brick house on a street made up of many other brick houses in a long row like giant beads on a string." There were also two older sisters and a brother in the family, but Mary Effie and Consuelo were near the same age and their interests were similar.

The family enjoyed books, so there were good times in the red brick house. Mary Effie's mother read to the two younger girls regularly, Bible stories, poetry, fairy tales, and many children's magazines that came by mail to their home. The two little girls enjoyed all kinds of stories, but books about the ways of nature were their favorites. They never tired of listening to factual material that explained the out-of-doors, described trees and flowers, or told of the habits of all sorts of animals.

Mary Effie and Consuelo liked to lie on the floor with their paints beside them, drawing flowers, trees, and birds.

Consuelo was fond of singing and playing the piano. "But I liked to write," Mary Effie has related. "I began writing verses at the age of five, and when I was eleven years old, I wrote a novel of four pages and three chapters!"

When Mary Effie was seven years old her father was elevated to the office of Bishop in his Church, and the family left their red brick house in Philadelphia and moved first to Texas, where they lived for four years, and later to their permanent home in Xenia, Ohio. Mary and Consuelo continued to enjoy their painting, drawing and music, but Mary Effie thought often of her friends and her old home in Philadelphia. She missed them all, particularly the organ grinder with his cunning little monkey that amused the children so. She pictured them in her mind constantly, and one day she wrote a poem about the organ grinder.

> I had some pennies for the store
> The organ man came near our door,
> He played a little jumpy tune,
> I gave him all my pennies soon.

The children were encouraged to continue their drawing, painting and writing, but Mary Effie, who says she had no singing voice, anyway, worked hardest at trying to write, mostly verses.

After high school, Mary Effie attended Wilberforce University, a Methodist Institution in Xenia, Ohio. She continued working in the Church and Sunday School, where she tried always to help the children "appreciate nature and God's creatures." She also attended Oberlin College in Ohio and the University of Pennsylvania, where her "work was well-rated," she says.

In 1920, she married a minister, the Reverend Henry Nesby Newsome. She decided to drop the Mary in her name. "Because four names in a row would be like the long row of houses on our street in Philadelphia," she said. She is now known as Effie Lee Newsome.

Effie Lee has always "worked in and out of the world of books." For eleven years she was head of the Children's Library in the Department of Education at Central State College in Wilberforce, Ohio. She helped and encouraged many of the students who were training to be teachers and professional leaders by introducing them to good literature. She worked with the librarians in the community of Xenia, in the churches, reading poetry and encouraging young people —and older people as well—to read good books. She says, "I enjoy working with all people of all ages, finding all interesting in some distinct way."

Effie Lee is an inveterate bird-watcher, never tiring of observing nest-building, and wondering about the "amazing journeys without road maps" that migrating birds take. She was invited by Carter G. Woodson, eminent Negro historian, author, and founder of The Association for the Study of Negro Life and History, to contribute some of her poems to *The Negro History Bulletin,* which he published. This organization later published her children's book, *Gladiola Garden,* a collection of verse.

She is also the author of *Come Ye Apart,* a book of her verse published by the Indianapolis Inter-racial Missionary Association. Her poems are included in eight adult anthologies, which are among the most representative of all the anthologies of Negro poetry.

Effie Lee retired from active duty in the library of the

College of Education at Wilberforce University in 1963, but she is still busy with her writing.

Mrs. Newsome's poetry helps children to see the beauty in nature and in the familiar world around them. Everyday things—food, flowers, birds, trees—are all included in her poems.

SKY PICTURES

Sometimes a right white mountain
Or great soft polar bear,
Or lazy little flocks of sheep
Move on in the blue air.

The mountains tear themselves like floss
The bears all melt away.
The little sheep will drift apart
In such a sudden way.

New polar bears appear
And roll and tumble on again
Up in the skies so clear.
The polar bears would like to get
Where polar bears belong.
The mountains try so hard to stand
In one place firm and strong.
The little sheep all want to stop
And pasture in the sky,
But never can these things be done,
Although they try and try!

SASSAFRAS TEA

The Sass'fras tea is red and clear
In my white china cup
So pretty I keep peeking in
Before I drink it up.

I stir it with a silver spoon
And sometimes I just hold
A little tea inside the spoon,
Like it was lined with gold.

It makes me hungry just to smell
The nice hot sass'fras tea
And that's one thing I really like
That they say's good for me.

ARNA BONTEMPS

[1902–   ]

At the height of what was called "The Negro Renaissance," twenty-one-year-old Arna Bontemps arrived in New York to teach, to saturate himself with the music he loved, to get his fill of good theater, and, "God willing, to become a writer!" God must have been more than willing, for Bontemps has become one of our foremost Negro writers—poet, novelist, dramatist, author of children's books, as well as many scholarly articles which have appeared in a wide variety of professional and literary magazines.

Arna Bontemps was born in Alexandria, Louisiana, on October 13, 1902, the son of Paul Bismarck Bontemps, a brickmason, whose father and grandfather had been brickmasons before him, and Marie Caroline (Pembrooke) Bontemps. His mother taught school before her marriage. When Arna was three, the family moved to Los Angeles, California. His mother died when he was twelve years old.

Arna Bontemps attended San Fernando Academy from 1917 to 1920; received his B.A. from the Pacific Union College, in Augwin, California, in 1923. While going to school, he earned money as a newsboy, gardener, postal clerk, and jubilee singer. He considered being a doctor or having a musical career, but sixteen months after graduating from college, when he was twenty-one, he went to Harlem (New York) to "see what all the excitement was about."

The area was in the upsurge of what was then known as the "Harlem Renaissance." To keep himself alive he taught school, but he expended quite as much energy evenings and weekends on his writing. Magazines like the *Crisis*, published by the National Association for the Advancement of Colored People, were printing his poems as early as 1924. In 1926, he took the Alexander Pushkin Award for his poem in free verse, *Golgotha is a Mountain*.

Golgotha is a mountain, a purple mound
Almost out of sight.
One night they hanged two thieves there,
And another man.
Some women wept heavily that night;
Their tears are flowing still. They have made a river;
Once it covered me.
Then the people went away and left Golgotha
Deserted.
Oh, I've seen many mountains;
Pale purple mountains melting in the evening mists
And blurring on the borders of the sky.
There are mountains in Africa, too.
Treasure is buried there;
Gold and precious stones
And moulded glory,
Lush grass is growing there
Sinking before the wind.
Black men are bowing.
Naked in that grass

Digging with their fingers.
I am one of them:
Those mountains should be ours.
It would be great
To touch the pieces of glory with our hands.
These mute unhappy hills,
Bowed down with broken backs,
Speak often one to another:
"A day is as a year," they cry,
"And a thousand years as one day."
We watched the caravan
That bore our queen to the courts of Solomon;
And when the first slave traders came
We bowed our heads.
"Oh, Brothers, it is not long!
Dust shall yet devour the stones
But we shall be here when they are gone."
Mountains are rising all around me.
Some are so small they are not seen;
Others are large.
All of them get big in time and people forget
What started them at first.

Oh the world is covered with mountains!
Beneath each one there is something buried:
Some pile of wreckage that started it there.
Mountains are lonely and some are awful.

    .   .   .

One day I will crumble.
They'll cover my heap with dirt and that will make a
    mountain.
I think it will be Golgotha.

While Arna Bontemps was teaching and writing poetry, publishing it in magazines and later in anthologies, he was also experimenting with other forms of writing. In 1931, his first novel, *God Sends Sunday*, gave him a new direction. He would write prose now, but he never abandoned his first "love," poetry.

He had won a first prize in a poetry contest sponsored by *The Crisis* magazine, in 1927, for his *Nocturne at Bethesda*, in which he seems to have put his whole heart and soul. These are the last two stanzas of the poem.

> I may pass through centuries of death
> With quiet eyes, but I'll remember still
> A jungle tree with burning scarlet birds,
> There is something I have forgotten, some precious
>   thing.
> I shall be seeking ornaments of ivory,
> I shall be dying for a jungle fruit.
>
> You do not hear, Bethesda.
> O still green water in a stagnant pool!
> Love abandoned you and me alike.
> There was a day you held a rich full moon
> Upon your heart and listened to the words
> Of men now dead and saw the angels fly.
> There is a simple story on your face;
> Years have wrinkled you. I know, Bethesda!
> You are sad. It is the same with me.

All around him the "Harlem Renaissance" was dying out, but at twenty-nine, Arna Bontemps was feeling a tremendous vitality and creativity. His novels came, one after another:

Black Thunder (1936), a remarkably vivid picture of the slave revolt led by a black man, Gabriel Prosser, and the terrible thunder-storm that ended the revolt. This was followed in 1939 by *Drums at Dusk*, a novel of slave revolt under Toussaint L'Ouverture, a successful venture in the time of Napoleon. The theme of both of these two novels is perhaps expressed very fittingly in his poem, *The Daybreakers*.

> We are not come to wage a strife
>   With swords upon this hill;
> It is not wise to waste the life
>   Against a stubborn will.
> Yet would we die as some have done:
> Beating a way for the rising sun.

God Sends Sunday, another novel, which dropped silently into the literary scene in that year of Depression, has since made its mark as a play and as a musical comedy, called *St. Louis Woman*.

Perhaps because, as a boy, books had had such a great influence on his life, Arna Bontemps began to write for boys and girls. Among the best known of these are: *Popo and Fifina* (1932), written in collaboration with Langston Hughes, a story of two Negro children in Haiti; *Sad-Faced Boy* (1937); *The Fast Sooner Hound* (1942), a tale about a hound that could outrun a railroad train, written with Jack Conroy; *Chariot in the Sky* (1951), a stirring account of the Fisk Jubilee Singers and of the beginning of Negro education during the Reconstruction era; and, perhaps best of all, *Lonesome Boy* (1955), a perceptive fantasy for teen-agers.

Arna Bontemps did not stop with writing fiction, and poetry. His *Story of George Washington Carver* (1954), a most popular biography of the great Negro scientist, is written for beginning readers. *Frederick Douglass, Slave, Fighter, Freeman* (1959), is an inspiring presentation of the famous orator and abolitionist; *Story of the Negro* is a stirring, yet accurate, history of the Negro, which won the Jane Addams Book Award in 1956. *One Hundred Years of Negro Freedom* is his latest book, celebrating the centennial of the signing of the Emancipation Proclamation in 1863.

With Langston Hughes, he edited the anthology, *The Poetry of the Negro, 1746–1949,* which contains not only the best of the poetry written in the Americas, but also that of Negro poets living outside the United States of America. Another collection young people will enjoy is *The Book of Negro Folklore,* prepared in collaboration with Langston Hughes, a definitive selection that is most unusual. His *Golden Slippers,* an anthology of poetry by Negroes selected especially for younger readers, is a classic in its field. He brings all his anthologies up-to-date in *American Negro Poetry* (1963).

Arna Bontemps expresses his own feelings, his philosophy and deep concern for all mankind in the following poem, *A Black Man Talks of Reaping.*

I have sown beside all waters in my day.
I planted deep, within my heart the fear
That wind or fowl would take the grain away.
I planted safe against this stark, lean year.

I scattered seed enough to plant the land
In rows from Canada to Mexico
But for my reaping only what the hand
Can hold at once is all that I can show.

Yet what I sowed and what the orchard yields
My brother's sons are gathering stalk and root,
Small wonder then my children glean in fields
They have not sown, and feed on bitter fruit.

His aim, he says, "is to keep poetry alive, to promote its enjoyment. . . . The way to promote the enjoyment of poetry is to read and enjoy it ourselves. The way to keep poetry alive is to stay alive ourselves."

This is also expressed very beautifully in *A Note of Humility*.

When all our hopes are sown on stony ground,
And we have yielded up the thought of gain,
Long after our last songs have lost their sound,
We may come back, we may come back again.

When thorns have choked the last green thing we loved,
And we have said all that there is to say,
When love that moved us once leaves us unmoved,
Then men like us may come to have a day.

For it will be with us as with the bee,
The meager ant, the sea gull and the loon:
We may come back to triumph mournfully
An hour or two, but it will not be soon.

Arna Bontemps has received many awards, among them the *Crisis* Poetry Prize, 1926; the Alexander Pushkin Poetry Prizes, 1926 and 1927; the *Opportunity* (Journal of Negro Life) Short Story Prize, 1932; two Julius Rosenwald Fellowships, 1938–1939 and 1942–1943; and the Jane Addams Children's Book Award, 1956. He received his M.A. degree from the University of Chicago in 1943.

Since 1943, this outstanding author has been Chief Librarian at Fisk University in Nashville, Tennessee, from which his wonderful poetry and stories have continued to pour forth. Among his latest books are two widely contrasting in subject matter but both sensitively interpretive—a collection of his own poems titled *Personals* and a group of brief biographies, *Famous Negro Athletes*.

Arna Bontemps is married to Alberta Johnson Bontemps. They have six children. One son, Paul, is an educator and youth worker in New York City, and a daughter, Joan, is a Librarian in Tennessee.

LANGSTON HUGHES

[1902–   ]

Langston hughes is one of the best known and best-loved poets in America. He is a poet for all the people because his verses appeal to young as well as older readers.

He was born in Joplin, Missouri, on February 1, 1902. His parents were Carrie Mercer and James Nathaniel Hughes, but they were soon separated, so his early life was spent with his mother in Kansas, first in Lawrence, then later in Topeka. She took him to see all the plays that came to town: *Uncle Tom's Cabin, Buster Brown, Under Two Flags*, and many others. His grandmother lived nearby and he liked to visit her because she told him wonderful and thrilling stories about his grandparents.

After he moved with his mother to Cleveland, Ohio, he said, "I was unhappy for a long time and very lonesome; then it was that books began to happen to me and I began to live in the wonderful world of books."

Langston attended Central High School in Cleveland with boys and girls of many nationalities. He was on the track team and, once in a while, his name appeared on the honor roll for scholarship. He discovered the poetry of Vachel Lindsay, Carl Sandburg, Edgar Lee Masters and Amy Lowell, and along

69

with other students, began writing verse for the school maga-zine, *The Belfry Owl*. He also sent his work to various national magazines hoping for publication.

The first poems he tried to write were without rhyme. Later, he attempted to compose verse about love and about the slums where many of his classmates lived. He read the poetry of Paul Laurence Dunbar. This helped him to appreci-ate the Negro dialect, and he tried to write poetry in dialect. Langston Hughes has captured the flavorsome speech of the Negro in a style quite different from the dialect of Dunbar, as is shown in this very moving poem called *Mother To Son*.

Well, Son, I'll tell you:
Life for me ain't been no crystal stair.
It's had tacks in it,
And splinters,
And boards torn up,
And places with no carpet on the floor—
Bare.
But all the time
I'se been a-climbin' on,
And reachin' landin's,
And turnin' corners,
And sometimes goin' in the dark
Where there ain't been no light.
So, Boy, don't you turn back.
Don't you set down on the steps
'Cause you finds it's kinder hard.
Don't you fall now—
For I'se still goin', honey,
I'se still climbin',
And life for me ain't been no crystal stair.

During his high school years he read avidly, both prose and poetry—Dreiser, Edna Ferber, Schopenhauer, Nietzsche, de Maupassant in French, and many other authors. He spent many hours in the Cleveland Public Library. While there, he became acquainted with Effie Power, a distinguished children's librarian, who encouraged him to read widely and write poetry. She wrote an introduction to his first book of poems for young people, *The Dream Keeper*, published in 1932.

Langston Hughes spent the summers with his father in Mexico, where he earned money by tutoring members of wealthy Mexican families who were unable to speak English.

One of his best known poems was written on the train en route to Mexico. Lonely and unhappy about having to spend the summer away from his friends, he looked out of the train window and noticed the muddy Mississippi River, which reminded him of what he had read about the history and early beginnings of the Negro race in Africa and in the United States. So he began putting down his ideas on the back of an old envelope taken from his pocket. The entire poem was rewritten on a single sheet of paper with very few corrections or very little re-writing. It is included in many anthologies of American poetry and is called *The Negro Speaks of Rivers*.

I've known rivers:
I've known rivers ancient as the world and older than the
    flow of human blood in human veins.

My soul has grown deep like the rivers.

I bathed in the Euphrates when dawns were young,
I built my hut near the Congo and it lulled me to sleep.
I looked upon the Nile and raised the pyramids above it.

71

I heard the singing of the Mississippi when Abe Lincoln went
down to New Orleans, and I've seen its muddy bosom
turn all golden in the sunset.

I've known rivers:
Ancient, dusky rivers.

My soul has grown deep like the rivers.

After graduating from Central High School in Cleveland,
Langston Hughes enrolled at Columbia University in New
York City, in 1921, and spent a year there. To finance his
college education, he signed up to work on a freighter during
the summer of 1923 and, instead of returning to college, he
spent the year 1924 in Paris, working as a doorman, waiter,
cook, and at other odd jobs. He then went to Italy, spending
eight weeks there, after which he worked his way home on a
freight steamer.

He went to Washington, D.C., and worked in the office of
Carter G. Woodson, noted Negro historian and author, who
published *The Journal of Negro History*, *The Negro History
Bulletin*, and many other books and periodicals about the
Negro's history. Langston found the work interesting but the
salary very low in Dr. Woodson's office, so he left there and
worked as a bus boy in a Washington hotel. One day in the
hotel dining room, he saw one of the poets he admired most,
Vachel Lindsay. Langston left three of his poems at Vachel's
table with a note and the poet read the note and the verses.
He shared the poems by reading them aloud to an audience
that night, then sent Langston a letter, encouraging him to
keep on writing and to continue to send the results of his
efforts to publishers.

Following this morale-boosting advice, Langston submitted his poems to all the leading magazines, some of which were accepted, while others were sent back. However, many of those returned were accompanied by letters of encouragement.

Langston puts his feelings about racial discrimination into this poem, written especially for children. It is called *Merry-Go-Round; Colored Child at Carnival.*

> Where is the Jim Crow section
> On this merry-go-round,
> Mister, cause I want to ride?
> Down South where I come from
> White and colored
> Can't sit side by side.
> Down South on the train
> There's a Jim Crow car.
> On the bus we're put in the back—
> But there ain't no back
> To a merry-go-round!
> Where's the horse
> For a kid that's black?

Langston Hughes entered Lincoln University in Pennsylvania to continue his college education. While there, he won the Witter Bynner Prize for undergraduate poetry. He graduated in 1929. He also wrote his first novel, *Not Without Laughter*, in that year. Later, this won for him the Harmon Gold Medal for Literature.

He received a Guggenheim Fellowship in 1935; a Rosenwald Fellowship in 1941; an American Academy of Arts and Letters Grant in 1947; and the Ainsfield-Wolfe Award in 1953. In 1960, he received the Spingarn Medal from the

NAACP for his contribution to American Literature. He writes a weekly column in *The New York Post*. This column often talks through a fictional character named "Simple," a Negro laborer who speaks his opinion on local, national, and world affairs in a Negro vernacular. He offers "earthy" advice on any and all subjects, and has grown to be a real person for many of Hughes' readers. Four volumes of prose about "Simple" have been published: *Simple Speaks His Mind*, (1950), *Simple Takes a Wife*, (1953); *Simple Stakes a Claim* (1957), and *The Best of Simple* (1961). *Simply Heavenly*, a play published in 1957 which is widely performed, is also about the homespun philosopher.

In 1963, Langston Hughes was honored with a second doctorate in Literature, conferred by Howard University. In 1964, Western Reserve University also gave him a Litt. D. On the concert stage his lyrics, set to music, have been performed by America's greatest Negro artists, Marian Anderson, Roland Hayes, Lawrence Winters, and many others.

Langston Hughes' poems have been translated into Chinese, Dutch, French, German, Japanese, Russian, and other languages. In addition to his poetry, he has written novels, operas, plays, and operettas. He is always in demand as a lecturer on Negro life and literature. He reads his poems for students and teachers in colleges and universities and lecture halls all over the world.

COUNTEE CULLEN

[1903-1946]

Countee cullen, one of America's most gifted young poets, was born in New York City on May 30, 1903, and grew up, an only child, in the parsonage of a Methodist Church in that city. He probably rebelled against the strict discipline which a minister's son is compelled to follow and, no doubt, this accounts for his lifelong fight against binding conformity.

His youth was sheltered and discloses nothing eventful or adventurous. As a boy, he had a lively and penetrating curiosity about life, and this quality in him is the mainspring of nearly all his poetry. In high school, his interest centered in poetry and his serious verses soon attracted the attention of his teachers.

After graduating from high school, Countee entered New York University. There, in 1925, he won the Witter Bynner Poetry Prize, in a contest open to all undergraduate students in all American colleges. He received a Master's degree from Harvard in 1926. Later, he became a teacher in the New York Public schools, where he remained until his death in 1946.

Countee Cullen's first book of poetry, *Color*, was published in 1925, when he was only twenty-two years of age. This won for him the coveted Harmon Gold Award for Literature.

Critics everywhere praised the work. This volume contains one of his most famous poems for young people, *Incident.*

> Once traveling in Old Baltimore
> Heart-filled, head filled with glee,
> I saw a Baltimorean
> Keep looking straight at me.
>
> Now I was eight and very small
> And he was no whit bigger
> And so I smiled, but he poked out
> His tongue, and called me, "Nigger."
>
> I saw the whole of Baltimore
> From May until December
> Of all the things that happened there
> That's all that I remember.

In 1927, Countee Cullen wrote and had published *Ballad of a Brown Girl*, and in the same year *Copper Sun* appeared. While he was in France on a Guggenheim Fellowship in 1929, he wrote *The Black Christ*. He traveled to England, where he wrote an article for *The Crisis* magazine, entitled "Countee Cullen in England," in which he gave his impressions of the English people who befriended him.

He met Winifred Cramps and John Fletcher and some of the other leading Quakers or Friends as they prefer to be designated, of England, who helped to arrange some programs of poetry reading in towns outside London. He read his poems to groups in Oxford, Bristol and Sydenham. Their response to his poetry and to him as a poet was warm and sincere.

Winifred Holtby, an English novelist, introduced Countee

to some of the journalists who published a few of his poems in English periodicals. He also met John Galsworthy and May Sinclair, both noted novelists. These literary people he called his friends because, through them, he was made to feel the warmth of the English writers. He went to the United States but returned again and again to England and each visit was met with the same cordiality and sincerity. He wrote of his visits, "I am surprised to learn how charming the English can be and how effortless that charm can appear." His wife, Mrs. Ida Cullen Harper, recalls that each summer after the close of school, he traveled abroad to study and write.

Countee Cullen was a dedicated teacher as well as poet, and he loved Paris. There he found many of his former students. One young man in particular, whom he had "flunked" in French, looked him up to thank him for the failure. He explained that, because of it, he had studied harder, went on to major in French and was then working as an interpreter for the French Government.

In 1927, Cullen edited *Caroling Dusk, an Anthology of Verse*, by Negro poets, published by Harper. In this anthology he included the poems of nearly forty Negro American poets. He says in the Introduction, "The place of poetry in the cultural development of a race or people has always been one of importance; indeed poets are prone, with many good reasons, to hold their art the most important."

Countee Cullen has been described as a "gentle poet" and as a "classroom poet." Unlike Langston Hughes, he did not want to be described as a "Negro poet." He wanted to be remembered as an *American* poet, writing about America. He is often quoted as saying, "I wish any merit that may be in my work to flow from it solely as the expression of a poet—with no racial consideration to bolster it up."

His poetry does indeed stand on its own merit as American poetry. He was an American poet who wrote beautiful poetry about life as he felt it. At the same time, he was proud of his Negro heritage as this poem shows:

BLACK MAJESTY
A Sonnet

(After reading John W. Vandercook's chronicle
of sable glory)

These men were kings, albeit they were black,
Christophe and Dessalines and L'Ouverture;
Their majesty has made me turn my back
Upon a plaint I once shaped to endure.
These men were black, I say, but they were crowned
And purple-clad, however brief their time.
Stifle your agony; let grief be drowned;
We know joy had a day once and a clime.
Dark gutter-snipe, black sprawler-in-the-mud,
A thing man did a man may do again.
What answers filter through your sluggish blood
To these dark ghosts who knew so bright to reign?
"Lo, I am dark, but comely," Sheba sings.
"And we were black," three shades reply, "but kings."

This poem was taken from *The Black Christ and other Poems*, published in 1929 by Harper and Brothers.

Cullen collaborated with Arna Bontemps in the dramatization of *St. Louis Woman*, from Bontemp's novel, *God Sends Sunday*, which was published in 1931. He wrote one novel, *One Way to Heaven*, (1932) and two books of poems composed especially for children, *The Lost Zoo*, (1940) and *My Nine Lives and How I Lost Them* (1942). These rollicking verses may be read aloud and enjoyed by young people, their elders, and little children, too. *On These I Stand* was published posthumously in 1947.

MARGARET WALKER

[1915-   ]

M ARGARET WALKER was born July 7, 1915, in Birmingham, Alabama, surrounded by books and music. Her father was a Methodist minister who owned an extensive library covering a great variety of subjects. Her mother, a musician, also loved and owned many books. In addition to Margaret, there were two sisters and a brother in the family.

Sensitive Margaret Walker wrote later of an impression she received when she was five years old. "I was busy discovering my world and it was a place of happiness and delight. Then one day a white child shouted in my ears 'nigger' and I was startled. I had never heard the word before. I went home and asked what it meant and my parents looked apprehensively at each other as if to say, 'It's come!' Clumsily, without adding hurt to the smart I was already suffering, they sought to explain, but they were unable to destroy my pain. I did not know why I was suffering, what brought this vague unease, this clutching for understanding."

As she grew older, such questions continued to trouble Margaret. She tried to find the answers in books about Negroes, but those in her schools, she said, "glorified the white race and described all Negroes as clowns or beasts." She tried to comprehend the segregated churches, hospitals, cemeteries and schools. "Some day," she whispered to herself, "I will find the answer and I will do something about it. I will write some books about people who have colored faces—books that will not make me ashamed when I read them."

Before Margaret was ten years old she knew about the inequities that existed between whites and Negroes. She tells us, "I knew what it was to step off the sidewalk to let a white man pass, otherwise he might knock me off. I was also accustomed to riding in Jim Crow street cars."

Once, Margaret and her mother climbed the fire escape to see a movie because there was no Negro entrance to the theater, and another time, she says, "My mother and I stood for hours upstairs in a darkened theater to hear a recital by Rachmaninoff because there were no seats for colored. . . . As an adolescent," she relates, "I wrote every single day I lived. It was like eating and sleeping and breathing, I guess. I wanted to express the feeling of the Negro people and my own especially."

As a minister's daughter, she learned to adjust readily to new surroundings and make friends easily. In each place where her father was assigned, she found fresh things to write about. Her poem *Childhood*, is an expression of her deep feelings.

> When I was a child I knew red miners
> dressed raggedly and wearing carbide lamps.
> I saw them come down red hills to their camps
> dyed with red dust from old Ishkooda mines.
> Night after night I met them on the roads,
> or on the streets in town I caught their glance;
> the swing of dinner buckets in their hands,
> and grumbling undermining all their words.

I also lived in low cotton country
where moonlight hovered over ripe haystacks,
Or stumps of trees, and croppers' rotting shakes
with famine, terror, flood, and plague near by;
where sentiment and hatred still held sway
and only bitter land was washed away.

Margaret attended schools in Meridian, Mississippi, and Birmingham, Alabama, and she graduated from Gilbert Academy in New Orleans, Louisiana, in 1930. When she was sixteen years old, she met Langston Hughes, the eminent Negro poet and writer. He was on a tour of the South, reading his poetry and lecturing. He was also encouraging young people to write. Langston suggested that Margaret send some of her work to the Negro magazines, so she began mailing her poems to various Negro periodicals, and in 1931, *The Crisis*, national organ of the NAACP, accepted one of these entitled *I Want To Write, I Want to Write the Songs of My People*.

After her graduation from Gilbert Academy, Margaret's family decided to send her to Northwestern University, in Evanston, Illinois. She was shy and afraid, since she had never attended school with whites, and felt that she would be backward because of her Southern all-Negro training. But she was surprised to discover that many white people faced inequities also; those who were poor and unemployed suffered just as Negroes did.

She found that, in Evanston and nearby Chicago, she was refused service at certain restaurants; also, she couldn't live in some of the dormitories at Northwestern during the 1930's. As Margaret thought of these and other injustices, she was stirred to write more than ever.

She joined the Northwestern University Chapter of the

Poetry Society of America and continued to write. For many reasons, Margaret enjoyed life in "the North," as Chicago was known to those who lived in the South. Stimulated by many authors and artists who visited the city and the campus at Northwestern, she composed many poems and sent her efforts to all kinds of periodicals. She paid tribute to one of the best known and the best loved Negro educators in her poem *For Mary McLeod Bethune:*

> Great Amazon of God behold your bread
> washed home again from many distant seas,
> The cup of life you lift contains no less,
> no bitterness to mock you. In its stead
> this sparkling chalice many souls has fed,
> and broken hearted people on their knees
> lift up their eyes and suddenly they seize
> on living faith, and they are comforted.
>
> Believing in the people who are free,
> who walk uplifted in an honest way,
> you look at last upon another day
> that you have fought with God and men to see.
> Great Amazon of God behold your bread.
> We walk with you and we are comforted.

Upon receiving her Bachelor of Arts degree from Northwestern University in 1935, Margaret Walker decided that there were wider opportunities for a Negro writer in Chicago than in the South, so she stayed and began looking for a job. She found employment as a newspaper reporter, secretary, social worker, and magazine editor, and finally joined the Federal Writers' Project. There she met the famous author,

Richard Wright, as well as Arna Bontemps, Negro poet and librarian, and other struggling young people who lived in Chicago during those years. There were some white writers among those working on the project with Margaret. One was Jack Conroy, co-author with Arna Bontemps of *Fast-Sooner Hound*, a rollicking folktale. Stack-O-Lee, Molly Means and John Henry were some of the figures of popular legends they enjoyed discussing. Later, all of these characters found their way into Margaret's writings.

In 1939, Margaret entered the School of Letters of the University of Iowa. There she wrote a collection of poems that were so excellent they were accepted in place of the usual dissertation for her Master of Arts degree, which she received in 1940. *For My People*, her poem, which first appeared in *Poetry*, a magazine of verse, in 1937, later won for her the Yale University Series for Younger Poets Prize. It was published in 1942 by Yale University Press. This became the title poem in a collection of her verse. Some of these poems appeared first in *Poetry*, *Opportunity, a Journal of Negro Life* (no longer published), *Creative Writing, American Prefaces*, and other periodicals.

For My People is deep and sincere. It is written in "free verse," which means it does not rhyme as most poems do, but has a strong rhythmic beat. The words Margaret Walker uses are sonorous and majestic. The rhythm of the poem catches and holds the interest of young and old. It seems to have come from the words she heard in her father's sermons and from the Bible verses she learned as a child. In part it reads

Let a new earth rise. Let another world be born.
Let a bloody peace be written in the sky.
Let a second generation full of courage issue forth;

Let a people loving freedom come to growth.
Let a beauty full of healing and a strength
of final clenching be the pulsing in our spirits
and our blood. Let the martial songs be written,
let the dirges disappear. Let a race of men now
rise and take control.

This was intended as a prophecy for her race and it is very
stirring and inspiring.

Some of her poems are quite different. Take, for instance,
Big John Henry, which shows great understanding of some of
the folkways of her people, part of which follows:

This here's a tale of a sho-nuff man
Whut lived one time in a delta lan'.
His hand was big as a hog's fat ham
And he useta work for Uncle Sam.
His gums was blue, his voice was mellow
And he talked to mules, fellow to fellow.

In addition to John Henry, Margaret re-wrote many of the
other folk tales and legends of Negroes, including the eerie
ghost tales of "Old Molly Means who was a hag and a witch."
Through her verses, she tried to retell many of these so that
young people might understand something of the Negro's
heritage. In her poem, *Lineage*, Margaret pays a fitting tribute
to her forebears:

My grandmothers were strong
They followed plows and bent to toil.
They moved through fields sowing seed
They touched earth and grain grew

They were full of sturdiness and singing
My grandmothers were strong.

My grandmothers were full of memories
Smelling of soap and onions and wet clay
With veins rolling roughly over quick hands
They have many clean words to say.
My grandmothers were strong.
Why am I not as they?

Armed with many honors, Margaret Walker went out to teach. She spent 1941–1942 as a Professor of English at Livingstone College, in Salisbury, North Carolina. In 1943, she went to West Virginia State College as a member of the English Department. A Rosenwald Foundation Fellowship for Creative Writing was awarded her in 1944. She spent the year 1963–64 at the University of Iowa, on leave from her permanent position as Professor of English Literature at Jackson College in Jackson, Mississippi.

Margaret and her husband, Firnest James Alexander, an interior decorator, and their four children, Marion, James, Sigismund, and young Margaret, live in Jackson, where she continues to teach and to contribute her writings to many periodicals and newspapers.

GWENDOLYN BROOKS

[1917-   ]

THE PULITZER PRIZE FOR POETRY in 1949 was won by Gwendolyn Brooks of Chicago for her book *Annie Allen*. She thus became the first Negro to achieve this honor.

The poet was born in Topeka, Kansas, on June 7, 1917. Her parents, David and Keziah Brooks, moved to Chicago shortly after she was born. Her earliest memories center in her father's reading to her and her brother Raymond, who liked to paint also. Gwendolyn does not remember exactly when she wrote her first poem, but she does recall that poetry was a real part of her family's life. Both her parents enjoyed music and books, all of which played an important part in the life of this eager young girl.

She attended Forrestville Elementary School in Chicago, and was a frequent book borrower in the Forrestville Branch of The Chicago Public Library. There she sometimes showed her poems to the librarian who praised her work and often posted her poems on the library bulletin board, along with the notices of "Programs and Events in Chicago."

At the age of thirteen, Gwendolyn wrote a poem, *Eventide*, which was accepted by *American Childhood Magazine*. This encouraged her greatly and delighted the Brooks family. At seventeen, she began writing serious poems which were published periodically in a local newspaper.

She graduated from Englewood High School and entered Wilson Junior College, where she majored in Literature. In June 1934, she graduated from Wilson and immediately began to look for employment. She applied at the Illinois State Employment Service and was sent to work as a "secretary" for Dr. E. N. French, a "Spiritual Advisor," who already had several secretaries assisting him in his business of "advisor" to those unfortunate enough to be out of work, looking for a wife or a husband, or those in almost any other difficulty, either financial or personal. He also made special "pills and powders for the lovelorn, discouraged, ill or in need." Her job consisted of helping to write hundreds of letters to prospective "patients," and also aiding in the packing of the bottles of "love-drops," "potions," "pills and powders" to be mailed. When his "Assistant Pastor" left, Dr. French ordered Gwendolyn to assume the duties of the "Assistant." This she flatly refused to do and was immediately fired.

Although she lost this first job, it was not a complete failure, since it gave her a glimpse of a side of Negro life in Chicago with which she was totally unfamiliar. The Dr. French office was in the famous "Mecca Building," on South State Street, a structure housing several hundred of Chicago's most destitute families. Living there also were derelicts, dope fiends, and other shady characters. It was this knowledge which gave her the background for much of her early writing and which still provides material for current work.

She attended classes at The South Side Community Art Center. Here she met Mrs. Inez S. Boulton of *Poetry Magazine*, who encouraged her to enter the magazine's annual poetry competition. Her entry was awarded the Eunice Tietjen

Prize for Poetry in 1949.

Gwendolyn Brooks read a notice about a contest sponsored by The Midwestern Writers Conference at Northwestern University, and entered several of her poems. She won four awards! In August 1945, her first book of poems, *A Street in Bronzeville,* was published. This was only the beginning. The young poet began receiving many honors. She was selected by *Mademoiselle Magazine* as one of its "Ten Young Women of Year 1945." She was made a Fellow of the American Academy of Arts and Letters in 1946, and won a Guggenheim Fellowship for two straight years, 1946 and 1947.

In 1949, a book of her verse, *Annie Allen,* was published. This was given one of America's highest honors, the much-coveted Pulitzer Prize for Poetry, in 1950. After winning this award, Gwendolyn Brooks was besieged with requests to compose some poetry for children. She wrote *Bronzeville Boys and Girls,* published in 1956, from which the following verses were taken. Each poem in this delightful children's book is named for a girl or boy. The collection was written, she says, in a manner quite different from all her other books. She set herself the task of writing "a poem a day," in order to complete the book in time to make a deadline!

DE KOVEN

You are a dancy little thing,
You are a rascal, star!
You seem to be so near to me,
And yet you are so far.

If I could get you in my hands,
You'd never get away.

I'd keep you with me always.
You'd shine both night and day.

GERTRUDE

When I hear Marian Anderson sing,
I am a STUFFless kind of thing.

Heart is like the flying air.
I cannot find it anywhere.

Fingers tingle, I am cold
And warm and young and very old.

But, most, I am a STUFFless thing
When I hear Marian Anderson sing.

JIM

There never was a nicer boy
Than Mrs. Jackson's Jim.
The sun should drop its greatest gold
On him.
Because, when Mother-dear was sick,
He brought her cocoa in.
And brought her broth, and brought her bread.
And brought her medicine.
And, tipping, tidied up her room.
And would not let her see
He missed his game of baseball
Terribly.

Gwendolyn Brooks has lectured at leading universities throughout the country. She gives generously of her time to talk to children in schools and she encourages them to write by criticizing each poem submitted to her by a child. She now offers an annual prize of one hundred dollars, in four twenty-five-dollar savings bonds, for the best poem written by a girl or boy.

In 1962, she was invited by President John F. Kennedy, along with other leading poets, to read some of her poetry at a Poetry Festival at The Library of Congress, in Washington, D.C. There she met the poet Robert Frost, just before his death. He offered warm praise of her work.

She is currently conducting a Poetry Workshop at Columbia College in Chicago.

Gwendolyn is the wife of Henry Blakely. They have two children, Henry Jr., a member of The U.S. Armed Forces, and Nora, aged eleven, who writes poetry and plans to be a teacher.

BIBLIOGRAPHY

Bontemps, Arna. *American Negro Poetry*. New York. Hill and Wang, 1963.
Bontemps, Arna. *Golden Slippers*. New York. Harper and Brothers, 1941.
Bontemps, Arna. *Personals*. London, Paul Breman, 1964.
Brooks, Gwendolyn. *Annie Allen*. New York. Harper and Brothers, 1949.
Brooks, Gwendolyn. *The Bean Eaters*. New York. Harper and Brothers, 1961.
Brooks, Gwendolyn. *Bronzeville Boys and Girls*. New York. Harper and Brothers, 1956.
Brooks, Gwendolyn. *A Street in Bronzeville*. New York. Harper and Brothers, 1945.
Brown, Sterling, Editor. *The Negro Caravan*. New York. The Dryden Press, Publishers, 1941.
Brown, Sterling. *Southern Road*. New York. Harcourt, Brace and Company, 1932.
Cullen, Countee. *Ballad of a Brown Girl*. New York. Harper and Brothers, 1927.
Cullen, Countee. *The Black Christ*. New York. Harper and Brothers, 1929.
Cullen, Countee. *Caroling Dusk*. New York. Harper and Brothers, 1927.
Cullen, Countee. *Color*. New York. Harper and Brothers, 1925.
Cullen, Countee. *Copper Sun*. New York. Harper and Brothers, 1927.
Cullen, Countee. *The Lost Zoo*. New York. Harper and Brothers, 1940.
Cullen, Countee. *The Medea and Other Poems*. New York. Harper and Brothers, 1935.
Dunbar, Paul Laurence. *Complete Poems of Paul Laurence Dunbar*. New York. Dodd, Mead and Company, 1913.
Dunbar, Paul Laurence. *Little Brown Baby*. New York. Dodd, Mead and Company, 1940.
Dunbar, Paul Laurence. *Lyrics of Love and Laughter*. New York. Dodd, Mead and Company, 1903.
Dunbar, Paul Laurence. *Lyrics of Lowly Life*. New York. Dodd, Mead and Company, 1896.
Dunbar, Paul Laurence. *Lyrics of Sunshine and Shadow*. New York. Dodd, Mead and Company, 1905.
Dunbar, Paul Laurence. *Majors and Minors*. Toledo, Ohio, Hadley and Hadley, 1895.
Dunbar, Paul Laurence. *Oak and Ivy*. Dayton, Ohio. United Brethren Publishing House, 1893.
Hammon, Jupiter. *An Evening Thought: Salavation by Christ, with Penitential Cries*. Privately published. 1760.

Hammon, Jupiter. *A Winter Piece.* Privately published, 1872.

Harper, Frances E. W. *Poems on Miscellaneous Subjects.* Philadelphia. Privately published, 1854.

Harper, Frances E. W. *Sketches of Southern Life.* Philadelphia. Privately published, 1872.

Hughes, Langston. *The Dream Keeper.* New York. Alfred A. Knopf, 1932.

Hughes, Langston. *Fields of Wonder.* New York. Alfred A. Knopf, 1947.

Hughes, Langston. *Fine Clothes to the Jew.* New York. Alfred A. Knopf, 1927.

Hughes, Langston. *Langston Hughes' Reader.* New York. George Braziller, Inc., 1958.

Hughes, Langston. *Montage of a Dream Deferred.* Published by the Author, 1951.

Hughes, Langston, Editor. *New Negro Poets, U.S.A.* Bloomington, Indiana, Indiana University Press, 1964.

Hughes, Langston. *One-Way Ticket.* New York. Alfred A. Knopf, 1949.

Hughes, Langston, Editor. *Poems from Black Africa.* Bloomington, Indiana. Indiana University Press, 1964.

Hughes, Langston and Bontemps, Arna, Editors. *Poetry of the Negro, 1746–1949.* New York. Doubleday, 1949.

Hughes, Langston. *Selected Poems of Langston Hughes.* New York. Alfred A. Knopf, 1959.

Hughes, Langston. *Shakespeare in Harlem.* New York. Alfred A. Knopf, 1942.

Hughes, Langston. *The Weary Blues.* New York. Alfred A. Knopf, 1926.

Johnson, James Weldon. *Book of American Negro Poetry.* New York. Harcourt, Brace and Company, 1931.

Johnson, James Weldon. *Fifty Years and Other Poems.* Boston. The Cornhill Company, 1917.

Johnson, James Weldon. *God's Trombones.* New York. The Viking Press, 1927.

Johnson, James Weldon. *Saint Peter Relates an Incident.* New York. The Viking Press, 1930.

Kerlin, Robert T. *Negro Poets and Their Poems.* Washington, D.C. Associated Publishers, Inc., 1935.

Newsome, Effie Lee. *Gladiola Garden.* Washington, D.C. Associated Publishers, Inc., 1940.

Redding, J. Saunders. *To Make a Poet Black.* Chapel Hill, North Carolina, University of North Carolina Press, 1939.

Walker, Margaret. *For My People.* New Haven, Connecticut. Yale University Press, 1942.

Wheatley, Phillis. *Poems on Various Subjects, Religious and Moral.* Privately published, 1773.

INDEX

94

CHARLEMAE ROLLINS began her valuable work as a librarian in The Chicago Public Library in March, 1927. She was in charge of the Children's Department in The George C. Hall Branch from January, 1932, to July, 1963, when she retired. The fine help she offered in her chosen field and the wide and enduring influence that she had on the reading tastes and enthusiasms of the young people whom she served so well have been captured by one of those who "grew up in our Branch Library" and happily shared in this generous heritage. Gwendolyn Brooks, the only Negro Pulitzer Prize Winner, wrote this poem as a tribute to Charlemae Hill Rollins:

> Her gift is long delayed.
> And even now is paid
> In insufficient measure.
> Rhymeful reverence,
> For such excellence,
> Is microscopic treasure.
> NOTHING is enough
> For one who gave us clarity—
> Who gave us sentience—
> Who gave us definition—
> Who gave us her vision.

Mrs. Rollins has taught in such diverse places as Fisk University, Nashville, Tennessee; Human Relations Workshop, San Francisco State College, California; Department of Library Science, Rosary College, River Forest, Illinois; and a class in Children's Literature at Roosevelt University, Chicago, Illinois.

She has received the following special honors: American Brotherhood Award of the National Conference of Christians and Jews, 1952; Library Letter Award of the American Library Association, 1953; Grolier Society Award of ALA, 1955; Woman of the Year of Zeta Phi Beta, 1956; Honorable Member, Phi Delta Kappa (Teachers Sorority), 1959; Good American Award of The Chicago Committee of One Hundred, 1962; Negro Centennial Awards (in three areas), 1963; and Children's Reading Round Table Award, 1963.

While writing books and contributing articles to such periodicals as *ALA Bulletin, Junior Libraries, Elementary English*, etc., etc., Mrs. Rollins has found time to serve as President of Children's Services Division of ALA, 1957–58; Chairman, Children's Section of Illinois Library Association, 1953–54; Chairman, Newbery-Caldecott Awards Committee of ALA, 1956–57; and Chairman, Elementary Section of Illinois Unit of Catholic Library Association, 1953–54.

In her *Famous American Negro Poets* she offers to boys and girls a worthwhile part of her rich knowledge and experience.